The Military Life of

FREDERICK THE GREAT

OF PRUSSIA

THE "MILITARY LIVES" BY TREVOR N. DUPUY, COL., U.S. Army (Ret.)

Frederick the Great of Prussia.

The Military Life of

FREDERICK THE GREAT

OF PRUSSIA

by TREVOR NEVITT DUPUY,
Col., U.S. Army, Ret.

FRANKLIN WATTS, INC.
575 Lexington Avenue
New York, N.Y. 10022

Maps by Dyno Lowenstein

*This book is dedicated
to my grandson, Christopher*

Contents

ix

Foreword

Surprisingly there is—to the best of this author's knowledge—
no book-length military analysis in English of the combat
leadership of Frederick II of Prussia. Much has been written
about him, as a man as well as a soldier, in both German and
French. Carlyle's splendid biography, and a few shorter general
biographies (mostly translated), provide considerable coverage
of Frederick's activities in the First and Second Silesian Wars
and the Seven Years' War. But the authors are on unfamiliar
ground in dealing with technical aspects of military strategy,
tactics, doctrine, and organization. Either they avoid comment
on these matters, or they reveal their ignorance.

Theodore Ayrault Dodge, one of the greatest of American
military historians, had planned to complete his tremendous
Great Captains series with a three-volume military biography of
Frederick. Unfortunately, however, Dodge died before he could
complete the work. Nonetheless, Dodge's lecture-essay on
"Frederick," in his short book entitled *Great Captains*, is probably the finest monograph in English on the generalship of the
great King of Prussia. It was a major reference in the research
done for this book, particularly in its treatment of the Battle of
Leuthen.

xi

The most important reference was Frederick's own *Military Instructions*, and the introduction to that work by Brigadier General Thomas R. Phillips in his *Roots of Strategy*. Many of the quotations from Frederick's writings that appear in this book are based on General Phillips' valuable translations.

Particularly useful is Ludwig Reiners' biography, *Frederick the Great*, translated from the German by Lawrence P. R. Wilson. Several of the quotations from Frederick's writings, as they appear in this book, are based upon Reiners' work. Frequent reference was also made to British Colonel George T. Denison's *History of Cavalry*. One of the classic analyses of the operations of the Seven Years' War is the article on that subject by the noted British military author and historian General Sir Frederick N. Maude in the *Encyclopaedia Britannica*; with some exceptions this has provided the framework for the treatment of Frederick's part in that war, as it is presented in this book.

I took advantage of relevant research which I had done earlier, in company with R. Ernest Dupuy, in two other works: *Military Heritage of America* and *An Encyclopaedia of Military History*. Other books referred to include Carlyle's classic *History of Friedrich II of Prussia*, Edith Simon's *The Making of Frederick the Great*, Victor Thaddeus' *Frederick the Great, the Philosopher King*, and Count Alfred von Schlieffen's military masterpiece, *Cannae*.

T. N. DUPUY

Introduction

The personality, accomplishments, and genius of Frederick II of Prussia defy easy analysis. He was a sensitive, cultured intellectual, and at the same time a ruthless, coldhearted disciplinarian. As a man, Frederick was the soul of personal honor; as a monarch he was sly, treacherous, and untrustworthy in his dealings with allies as well as with enemies. Of particular importance to us in this military biography, he was one of the greatest generals who ever lived.

In many respects Frederick was a typical eighteenth-century monarch, and also a typical eighteenth-century soldier. Unlike his predecessor, Gustavus, and his successor, Napoleon, he accepted the military systems and methods of war of his time as he found them. But he recognized that eighteenth-century warfare was slow, ponderous, and lacking in imagination. So, to achieve mobility and speed he made a number of practical changes in the system. He provided imagination merely by the natural processes of one of the keenest, quickest intellects of history.

No general has ever had a more thorough understanding of military principles, or of the fundamentals of military leadership, as well as of the technical aspects of military affairs, than did Frederick the Great.* In peacetime he devoted great attention to assuring himself that every soldier and specialist in his army could perform every detail of his job. In wartime, however, he ignored the details, which he left to the men he had trained in peace. Instead, during combat, he devoted himself to the immense tasks of commanding an army in the field, controlling and planning the complete economic and manpower mobilization of a nation at war, and, at the same time, exercising all of his responsibilities as chief of state. To be done properly, each of these tasks should have required the full-time attention of a vigorous man, each with his own separate staff. Yet Frederick performed them all, assisted by a handful of administrative staff officers, clerks, and messengers. And he performed all of them more efficiently than they were done in any other nation of eighteenth-century Europe. Yet, surprisingly, even in the most arduous campaigns, he never allowed his official responsibilities to interfere with several hours of flute-playing and poetry composition every evening.

Frederick was indeed the Great, by any standard of comparison with other soldiers and monarchs of history. He was particularly outstanding when measured against other rulers and other generals of his day in qualities of courage, willpower, self-discipline, industry, tenacity of purpose, and military professional skill. Even while a relatively young man he was called "the Great" by his contemporaries, mainly because he habitually won battles under circumstances in which victory seemed

* See Appendix for a discussion of military principles and of the nature of military leadership.

xiv

impossible. Few generals have been so universally feared in battle by their opponents.

Yet Frederick lost more battles than any other Great Captain. In part this was because he faced greater odds than any other successful general has ever encountered, before or since. In part it was also due to an unpredictable streak of obstinacy which sometimes led him to take apparently senseless risks. But when he lost—whatever the cause—he showed unparalleled ability to recover and to prevent his enemies from taking advantage of the setback.

By his strong will and matchless industry, Frederick laid the foundation for modern Germany. Not only did he keep his small country intact in a war in which he was simultaneously fighting all four of continental Europe's great powers; in the process he raised Prussia itself to the status of a great power respected by all others.

As a person, Frederick is almost impossible to understand. He was at once charming, unpredictable, insulting, crude, and sensitive. We are repelled by his cruel habit of ridiculing people who could not possibly answer back. Sometimes he seemed to sacrifice brave men senselessly, with no indication of remorse or concern. He was vain, theatrical, and egotistical; he talked incessantly; he often blamed others for those few military losses that resulted from his own occasional fits of obstinacy. On the other hand, we know from his *Instructions* that, save in that secret document, Frederick never revealed his innermost thoughts and feelings. It is clear that even his most unpleasant and abhorrent characteristics were at least partly poses.

xv

Furthermore, Frederick had qualities—courage, resourcefulness, industry, persistence, intelligence, and complete objectivity—which preserved him and Prussia against almost unbelievable adversity.

Frederick himself said, summarizing his efforts before the
end of the Seven Years' War:

> I have all the properties of a stage hero—always in
> danger, always on the point of perishing. One must hope
> that the conclusion will come soon, and if the end of the
> piece be lucky, we will forget the rest.

The end of the piece *was* lucky—but it was luck forged and
used by one of the most indomitable, unconquerable men who
ever lived.

The Military Life of

FREDERICK THE GREAT
OF PRUSSIA

CHAPTER 1

Sentenced to Death

A Court-Martial Does Its Duty

Resplendent in his full-dress uniform, Lieutenant General Count von Schulenburg of the Prussian army, president of a specially convened court-martial, solemnly read to the other members a communication from King Frederick William of Prussia. There were fifteen officers sitting at the long table on either side of General von Schulenburg, ranging in rank from major general to captain. With eyes downcast they listened as their president read a strongly worded rebuke from the king. He wrote that their findings in a case involving his son, Crown Prince Frederick, and two other young Prussian officers, constituted "an act of perfidy."

The king reminded the court-martial that the prince and his two companions had been caught attempting to flee from Prussia. They were deserters from the Prussian army, and they may even have been engaged in a treasonable plot with the court of a foreign power. Desertion alone was a crime which warranted a cruel death. Thus the king approved the sentence of death *in absentia* for Ensign Karl von Keith, who had suc-

3

ceeded in escaping and fleeing the country. The sentence of life imprisonment which the court imposed upon Lieutenant Johan Hermann von Katte, however, was insufficient. The king ordered the court to review the evidence and "pronounce a different verdict." In other words, the king's letter was an order to the court to sentence von Katte to death.

Frederick William also rebuked the court for declaring itself incompetent to pass judgment on Prince Frederick Karl, simply because he was the Crown Prince of Prussia. The king ordered them to review the evidence in this case as well, reminding them that Frederick, a Prussian officer as well as a prince, had deserted from the army, an offense within the competence of the court. There is little doubt that the king wanted the sentence of death passed on his son, just as he was demanding it for Lieutenant von Katte.

Despite the letter from the king, the court repeated its original findings. Frederick William was furious. After hinting that he would find ways of "destroying those persons who have tried to side with my children against me," he ordered the military court to inform Lieutenant von Katte that, by royal decree, he was sentenced to death. Frederick William then added that, "though lawfully he should be torn with red hot pincers and hanged, . . . out of regard for his family" he would merely be beheaded instead.

It is not so clear how the king then handled the case of his son. Apparently, after dire threats to the members of the court-martial, the king again demanded that they reach a verdict on the desertion of the crown prince. There is no supporting record, but it seems that under royal pressure the court finally obeyed Frederick William's order; they found Prince Frederick guilty and imposed the verdict of the death penalty, but recommended mercy for the prince.

It is possible, however, that the king himself imposed a sentence of death on Frederick, as he had already done for von Katte. In any event, during the first week of November, 1730, the young prince languished in solitary confinement in the fortress of Küstrin, awaiting the executioner.

Early Years of Prince Frederick

Prince Frederick Karl Hohenzollern had been born at Potsdam nearly nineteen years earlier, on January 24, 1712. His father was Crown Prince Frederick William; the grandfather of the baby prince was Frederick I, who had been proclaimed the first King of Prussia in 1701.

The Hohenzollerns had been electors of Brandenburg, and later of Prussia, since the fifteenth century. As electors, they were leading princes of the Holy Roman Empire and one of the select group of German rulers responsible for electing the emperors. For his loyal support to the emperor in a war against France, Prince-Elector Frederick Hohenzollern had been granted the title of King of Prussia. As Frederick I, the new king set about making himself and his kingdom respected by the older monarchs of Europe. Most of these rulers regarded Prussia as a frontier outpost of the Hapsburg Empire, and

5

thought of its Hohenzollern family as crude upstarts. To change such opinions, Frederick established a royal court in Berlin and Potsdam, which was a copy of the French court of Louis XIV at Versailles.

Young Prince Frederick Karl had at least equally distinguished ancestors on his mother's side. Sophie Dorothea had been a princess of Hanover before she married Frederick William. She was descended from Mary Queen of Scots; her father was the Elector of Hanover, soon to become King George I of England.

The infant Prince Frederick Karl had three distinguished royal godfathers at his christening: Emperor Charles VI; Czar Peter the Great of Russia; and his grandfather, the Elector of Hanover. There were two other godfathers: a representative of the States General of Holland, and a representative from the Swiss Republic of Berne.

Thirteen months after the birth of Frederick Karl his grandfather, Frederick I, died. Frederick William became the second King of Prussia at the age of twenty-five; his baby son was now the crown prince. The new king quickly went about changing things in Prussia. He had not liked the way his father had copied the French court. He got rid of all the expensive elegance which had been Frederick I's pride—the servants in fancy dress, the powdered wigs, the diamonds, the rich food and beautiful silks, and also the elaborate court procedures, or protocol. The new king had two aims—a thrifty administration and a disciplined army. But in one thing he agreed with his father: he wished to gain greater respect for Prussia throughout Europe.

Europe, 1714, after the ascension of Frederick William of Prussia

The Prussian army was by far the most important thing in the life of King Frederick William. It was both his hobby and the chief means by which he planned to gain universal respect. He devoted close attention to all aspects of military affairs. It was typical of his interests that the king's closest associate was Prussia's greatest military hero, General Field Marshal Prince Leopold of Anhalt-Dessau. The king put Prince Leopold—known to history as "the Old Dessauer"—in charge of the army's training center at Potsdam.

The combined efforts of these two strict disciplinarians—king and field marshal—soon converted an army that was already good, into a superb instrument of war. But, despite two brief campaigns, Frederick William's new army had never really been tested in warfare. The king was not a person to make war, or practice aggression, and was content to build this magnificent fighting machine with little desire, apparently, to use it.

The one time that Frederick William actually sent his army into a major battle was in 1715, when Charles XII of Sweden tried to take Pomerania. The Old Dessauer led an allied force —Prussian, Danish, Saxon, and Russian—that defeated the smaller Swedish army at the Battle of Rügen.

Typical of the king's interest in the army as a hobby, rather than as an instrument of national policy, was his obsession with his Royal Guard. Every soldier in the guard was a strapping man over six feet tall. A principal duty of Prussian envoys in other countries was to seek giants, who were then to be enticed to go to Prussia to join the Royal Guard.

During the early years of his reign Frederick William loved to play with his little boy, Crown Prince Frederick—or "Fritz" as he called him. He took the boy everywhere. The king was certain that Fritz would turn out to be a soldier and a hunter. In his own lonely childhood the king had never had a brother to play with; now he looked forward to the day when the young prince could become that companion he had hoped for. At the age of seven the boy was taken away from his governess, and his education was supervised by men. The king appointed a tutor and assistant tutor from the army—Lieutenant General Finck von Finckenstein and Lieutenant Colonel von Kalkstein. The teaching of nonmilitary matters was done by a French Huguenot, Jacques Egid Duhan de Jandun. The king himself carefully planned the details of the boy's teaching and training; he established a firm schedule covering all of Fritz's waking hours.

Despite his care in placing the education of the young prince in the hands of men, and despite his own careful supervision, Frederick William had become very disappointed with the boy by the time he reached the age of nine. Fritz was showing interest in such things as French literature, music, art, and all of the subjects that the king disliked, or thought useless for the soldier-prince he wanted for a son. He was both displeased and jealous when he observed the affection of the boy for his mother, Queen Sophie Dorothea. Also annoying to the king was the fact that Frederick's closest associate was his sister Wilhelmina. The king wanted Fritz to like to play with boys, not with girls, not even his own sister.

9

Frederick William I reviews his giant Royal Guards. (New York Public Library)

Frederick William wanted Fritz to be more manly. Yet despite harsh punishment, the king could not break the boy's affection for his mother and his sister. Nor could he attract the boy's attention away from matters which he himself considered effeminate, and unbecoming for a soldier and a man. Particularly infuriating to the king was the boy's enjoyment in playing the flute.

When he was ten, Fritz wrote his first novel. By this time, Frederick William had decided his oldest son was worthless and his affections had been transferred to a new baby, Prince Augustus William. The king was depressed by the thought that he would be succeeded on the throne of Prussia by a cowardly, womanlike creature.

Unintentionally the queen added to the troubles between father and son. She had long been planning for English marriages for Fritz and Wilhelmina, to the son and daughter of the Prince of Wales, who soon became George II. Frederick William disliked George II, and furthermore he was under considerable pressure from Emperor Charles VI not to enter an alliance with England.

Humiliations, beatings, punishment of every form became the daily lot of young Frederick and Wilhelmina. When Frederick William discovered Frederick's collection of 3,700 books, he destroyed them all. The boy had been made an honorary colonel of a regiment, but when he was still in his early teens Frederick William demoted him to the rank of ensign. At mealtimes the king often came to the regimental mess, where he forced Frederick to sit at the foot of the table, and ridiculed him throughout the meal in front of the embarrassed officers.

The fact that the king mistreated his children in public brought the prince and princess sympathy from those around them as well as from the Prussian people. The meddlesome monarch was not well liked by his subjects. He had a passion for trifles, and interfered in every aspect of the daily lives of his people. They hated to see him coming in his travels around the country and through the cities. He had been known to inject himself into the quarrels of married couples; often he would beat a lazy farmer with his cane, and would even stop on the street to give advice to children, or to scold them. The king

11

treated his subjects, in fact, much as he did his son. As a result, the people developed an affection for the boy that neither the father nor the grandfather had ever had from the Prussians.

Another source of bitterness for the king was Frederick's lack of interest in the strict Lutheran faith to which Frederick William was wholeheartedly devoted. The boy showed interest in learning about the beliefs of other faiths, including Catholicism and Presbyterianism, both of which were detested by the king. Frederick William sometimes feared, in fact, that the crown prince was not even a sincere Christian.

Frederick William had gout, which may have been partly responsible for his evil temper and outbursts of brutality. He was also subject to moods of depression, and many people thought he was insane. He ate and drank to excess and, as time went on, became increasingly cruel as well as insulting to those around him.

By the time Frederick was seventeen, he had two close friends, young army officers, Ensign Karl von Keith and Lieutenant Johan Hermann von Katte. To them, as well as to Wilhelmina, he could confide his troubles. His life was becoming increasingly difficult and, being young, he lacked the patience to endure it until his father should die and he would be on his own as king. The prince dreamed of escape to England, where he felt he had allies and would have freedom.

Frederick frequently discussed this idea with his friends Keith and Katte, and also with his sister. The king, suspicious of all of his son's associates, sent Keith away to a remote post. Nevertheless, Frederick went ahead with escape plans with

Katte, planning to run to France and then Holland, from which he could go to England. There he expected to marry the Princess Amalia, as his mother had always hoped.

Attempt at Escape

An opportunity to put this plan into effect seemed to arise during the summer of 1730. Frederick William took a trip through most of Germany, and decided to take Frederick with him, to keep an eye on him. One officer, a Colonel von Rachow, was assigned to stay with the prince at all times, and never to let him out of his sight.

On August 4 the Prussian royal party stopped at Mannheim, on the Rhine River, not far from France. Frederick had obtained the assistance of a royal page, the younger brother of Karl von Keith. He told the youth to bring horses to his quarters before dawn the following morning, and they would ride to the French border. Early the next morning Frederick got up quietly, without awaking Colonel von Rachow, and went out to wait for the younger Keith. But just as Keith and the horses arrived, so did Colonel von Rachow.

In confusion, Frederick returned to his room, and Keith took the horses away. Surprisingly, Rachow did not report the incident to the king. He felt very sorry for the young prince who was so badly treated and denied all the normal pursuits of young men. But the strain was too much for the younger Keith. Fearful that he and Frederick would be betrayed, he felt he could save his life only by confessing the whole story to Frederick William. The enraged king placed his son under arrest. He put him under guard on board the royal yacht and sent him down the river to Wesel, for questioning on Prussian territory.

Somehow Frederick managed to get word to the older of the Keith brothers and to Katte that the plot had been discovered. He urged them to flee. Keith made good his escape to England, but Katte for some reason stayed in Berlin. Frederick William ordered that he be seized and thrown into prison.

There followed a period of intensive investigation. Frederick William was convinced that the attempted escape was part of an English plot to overthrow him and to place Frederick on the throne. At the first interrogation he drew his dagger, and in fury was about to plunge it into his son, but was restrained by some of his officers. He ordered Frederick to be taken to the fortress of Küstrin; he said he never wanted to see his son again. The guards escorting the prince to his prison were ordered to kill him rather than allow him to escape.

The investigation produced no evidence of any foreign plot. It was clear to everyone, except the king, that young Frederick had merely grown desperate under the inhuman treatment he was receiving, and was simply trying to get away from the cruelties of his father. Nonetheless, Frederick William ordered the court-martial to try the prince and his two friends for desertion. In his fury he was determined that his son must die. Meanwhile, Frederick was in solitary confinement at Küstrin— under constant observation by guards, who were forbidden to talk to him.

CHAPTER 2

The Education of a King

Küstrin

Word that Frederick William was planning to have his son executed spread quickly throughout Europe. In the days after the court-martial, in late October and early November, 1730, Frederick William received messages from many other rulers, urging him to be lenient with the prince.

The king at first ignored all of these appeals. It seems likely that by the beginning of November, however, he had already had second thoughts about having Frederick put to death. But he was determined that the young man should suffer the most severe punishment possible, short of death.

The first measure of this punishment was the worst, and the most cruel. Young von Katte was taken to Küstrin, and early on November 6 was beheaded under the window of the room where Frederick was imprisoned. Under orders from the king, the prince was forced to go to the window and observe the execution. Frederick fainted from grief and shock. For several days he was delirious, calling to Katte; frequently he thought he was talking to his friend who had died so bravely for him.

During this period of Frederick's grief the king sent his favorite churchman, Pastor Müller, to spend most of his time with the prince. Müller's mission was to convert the lad back from his doubtful religious beliefs to the true Lutheran faith of the king. Frederick, recovering from his delirium, finally realized what was happening. Pleased with an opportunity to talk to someone after nearly three months of solitary confinement, he showed signs of religious repentance. It is likely that he was merely pretending to respond to the sympathetic arguments of the churchman. Müller, however, sent reports to the king that the prince was truly repentant. He added his own pleas for mercy to those which Frederick William was receiving from all over Prussia and from foreign capitals.

The king had been suffering from insomnia during this period of strain. And on the few occasions that he could get to sleep, he was afflicted with nightmares. He was having doubts about the harshness of his original decisions. If he had not already decided to spare the prince, the reports from Pastor Müller finally caused him to relent. He released the prince from the sentence of death, and from his solitary confinement.

Frederick was allowed to leave the prison on November 20, and was returned to rank and title, although not allowed to wear a military uniform. He was assigned to a minor administrative job in a government bureau in Küstrin. Frederick William refused to see his son or to grant him pardon. The youth would have to serve a term of hard work as a government employee. Then, said the king, "provided he does it all with a good grace and goes on that way, there'll be a pardon."

Frederick's duties were carefully outlined by the king. He

was to sit in the Council Room of the Board of War and Domain Lands, listening to the meetings and copying papers for the members, from 7:00 to 11:30 A.M. and 3:00 to 5:00 P.M. daily. He was to attend church three times each Sunday. He could not have his flute, or listen to any music except hymns. There was to be no reading except for religious and administrative works. He could not go out, nor could he entertain.

Good reports flowed to the king from the director of the council. In fact, all of the prince's associates were truly impressed with his devotion to duty and steady hard work for long hours. They were also impressed by the quality of his work and the thoughtfulness of his reports. They did not know that he was writing hundreds of witty verses at night, and that he was also quietly making fun of them and of the work they were doing.

Pardon

Frederick first saw his father again on August 15, 1731, Frederick William's birthday, when the king stopped at Küstrin, while on a trip from Lithuania to Berlin. Frederick threw himself at his father's feet, while the king lectured him again on all of his faults and failures. But at the end of the interview Frederick William embraced his son.

After this royal visit, more liberties were granted to Frederick. He was allowed out of the city. He could visit factories and estates, with a pass from the governor, provided that young women were carefully excluded from the company. He was not yet allowed to see his mother or Wilhelmina. Above all, his appeals for readmittance into the army were disapproved. His father, "the Soldier King," regarded the wearing of the uniform as the greatest possible honor for any Prussian. To permit that would be a sign of complete reconciliation and pardon, and the king was not yet prepared to go that far.

However, the pardon came soon. On November 20, 1731, Frederick was allowed to attend the wedding ball of his sister Wilhelmina, who had been ordered by the king to marry the Margrave of Bayreuth.

Soon after this event, Frederick was also restored to the Prussian army, as colonel of a regiment of infantry in Ruppin. He was allowed to go to Ruppin, but in addition he was required to continue to work at administration at Küstrin. So he divided his time between the two places, devoting himself intensively to both his military and administrative duties, but without losing any of his keen wit. He continued to write verses in the evenings. Moreover, he resumed flute-playing, his favorite relaxation, and also was able to read in his new and growing library.

Marriage

Frederick was a confirmed bachelor. He saw himself as a future Philosopher King, a combination of Aristotle and Alexander the Great, spending time with learned men, as well as leading warriors, with no time for a wife or family. But Frederick William had other ideas. He believed that Frederick needed a good, steady German wife. The king decided that the best choice was Princess Elizabeth Christine of Brunswick-Bevern, niece of the emperor. This marriage had been suggested to the king by sly Austrian diplomacy; the court of Vienna believed that the empire and Austria needed an alliance with Prussia and its fine army.

Elizabeth Christine was not very attractive, and Frederick protested the engagement bitterly. But the king was determined. So Frederick reluctantly agreed, letting his father know the sacrifice he was making. He was by now completely realistic in his attitude toward his father. Whatever he may have felt or thought, he was completely obedient to his father's will, as the only practicable course.

Frederick was married on June 12, 1733, to Elizabeth Christine. The king gave the newlyweds a fine residence at Rheinsberg, in Ruppin. He finally released Frederick from his administrative duties at Küstrin. This German princess must have been quite important to Frederick William. Despite his normally miserly nature, the king spent a great deal on finery, dancing lessons, and things to make the girl happy and more charming to his obedient son.

Meanwhile war—the War of the Polish Succession—had broken out between France and the empire. Charles VI called upon his electors to provide contingents to support the Austrian army. During most of 1734 Frederick and his regiment were part of a Prussian contingent of 10,000 men operating under the great Prince Eugene in the Rhine Valley.

19

It was not much of a campaign. Eugene was old, and had lost his aggressive, fighting spirit. At the same time, the French were too respectful of the Austrian general's reputation to offer any real challenge. But there were a number of skirmishes; Frederick was several times under fire, and conducted himself well. The thing that most impressed Frederick during this campaign was the poor quality of the Austrian troops. He would remember this a few years later.

Frederick William spent one month at the front, rejecting comfortable quarters in favor of living in the field in the tents with his troops. He fell ill, and was for a while close to death, but then recovered. The war soon ended, and the troops returned home.

In 1734 Frederick began a correspondence with Voltaire. This led to a close friendship, and a continuous exchange of letters which was to last—with some interruptions—for forty-two years.

Reconciliation

In 1739, Frederick accompanied Frederick William on a tour of Prussian Lithuania—the northeasterly portion of East Prussia. He was impressed with his father's accomplishments, which had turned this area from a wasteland into a thriving and prosperous country. He began to appreciate his father's qualities as an administrator. He wrote enthusiastically to Voltaire about the changes which his father had made in Prussia during his reign.

In fact, although Frederick William was a tyrant and bully in his own family, as well as a meddler in the lives of the Prussian people, he had put his kingdom on a sound economic and political basis. He had built an army of 80,000 men which was recognized as one of the best in Europe. Prussia had no debts, and there was a full treasury to show for his frugality. He had established a sound central administration of his country, and he maintained it by incessant toil. He was the first ruler in Europe to adopt the idea of universal education. Trade was thriving. Frederick William had taken over a new and unsteady kingdom and made it sound; for all his faults and unpopularity he had constructed something for his people of which he and they could be proud.

Although Frederick William and Frederick had been reconciled with each other, the old hatred had continued beneath the surface of their relationship. Not until his last days did Frederick William ever believe that his son would be anything more than a good flute player and a bad poet. But, on May 28, 1740, he surprisingly said, "I die content with so worthy a son to succeed me."

Three days later Frederick William was dead. Frederick II became the third King of Prussia. Instead of the quiet, inexpensive burial ceremony his father requested, Frederick gave him a splendid and expensive funeral.

21

Frederick the Great, as a young man. (*Charles Phelps Cushing*)

The New King

As soon as Frederick was king, he instituted a series of innovations and reforms. While keeping the same tight control over administration and finances which his father had established, the new king tried to make life easier and more pleasant for his people. Torture was abolished; brutality in army discipline was forbidden—although discipline was not relaxed. Press censorship was lifted, complete religious tolerance was initiated, and the crown's hunting rights were reduced.

In September, Frederick published a book entitled *Anti-Machiavel*. In this he challenged the ruthless concepts of Machiavelli; he upheld the ideal of a liberal monarch and an enlightened rule.

If other European nations thought the new King of Prussia would be easier to deal with than his father, they soon learned better. Frederick disbanded his father's giant Grenadier Guard regiment as being too expensive; but he established sixteen new battalions of Prussian infantry. Then, in September, 1740, he took action to settle a drawn-out dispute between Prussia and the prince-bishop of Liège over the ownership of Herstal, a small town near Liège. Frederick William had offered to give up his claim to Herstal, in return for payment of 100,000 thalers. The bishop had refused, and Frederick William had fumed. But Herstal remained under the control of the bishop, who could count on the support of both France and the empire.

Frederick, however, sent an ultimatum to the bishop, to settle the case or render himself "responsible before the world for the consequences which will inevitably follow." When the bishop ignored the ultimatum, Frederick sent troops into Liège territory and exacted taxes which he claimed were owed by the inhabitants of Herstal. The alarmed bishop then agreed to pay Prussia 200,000 thalers for Herstal, if only Frederick would withdraw his troops. Frederick promptly agreed. He had settled the matter without bloodshed, at twice the price his father had hoped to gain from settlement.

CHAPTER 3

First Silesian War

Maria Theresa and the Pragmatic Sanction

On October 20, 1740, less than five months after Frederick had
ascended the throne of Prussia, the Holy Roman Emperor
Charles VI of Austria died. The emperor's death created a European crisis which he himself had long foreseen. Charles, the
last male of the imperial house of Hapsburg, had several children, but all were daughters. He had succeeded his elder
brother, Joseph I, as emperor, since Joseph also was without
male heirs.

Charles knew that a woman could never be elected to succeed him on the throne of the Holy Roman Empire. This did
not worry him greatly, however, since the empire was really only
a loose confederation of the kingdoms and principalities of
Germany. But he did want to be sure that his eldest daughter,
Maria Theresa, and her successors, would retain control of all
of the lands under Austrian control. These included the Grand
Duchy of Austria itself, plus the kingdoms of Hungary and Bohemia, and a number of other rich principalities and duchies
scattered throughout Europe. It was these far-flung Austrian

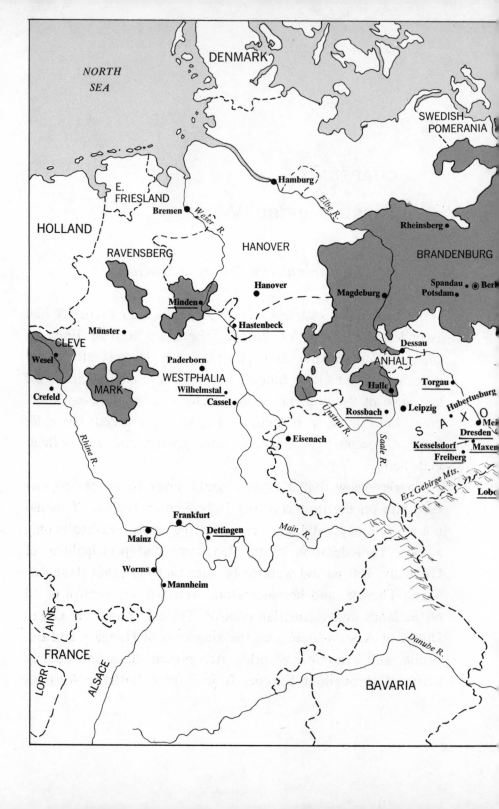

BALTIC SEA

POMERANIA

Königsberg

Gross Jägersdorf

EAST
PRUSSIA

Vistula R.

Warsaw

POLAND

Zorndorf
Küstrin
Kunersdorf
Frankfurt-on-Oder

Oder R. Kay

Görlitz Hennersdorf Parchwitz
Hochkirch Liegnitz Ohlau Breslau
Mays SILESIA
Striegau
Zittau Hohenfriedberg Bunzelwitz Brieg
Schweidnitz
Landshut Burkersdorf Strehlen Mollwitz
Grottkau Oppeln
Trautenau Neisse R.
Soor Glatz Neisse Klein
Schnellendorf
Chlumnetz UPPER
Königgrätz Sudeten SILESIA
Mts.
Elbe R.
gue AUSTRIAN SILESIA
Kolin
Chotusitz
Kuttenberg Czaslau
BOHEMIA Olmütz
Habern MORAVIA

HAPSBURG DOMINIONS

HUNGARY

AUSTRIA

PRUSSIA

Leuthen SITES OF BATTLES

0   50   100

Scale of Miles

z

Vienna

possessions, rather than the title of Emperor, which had made the Hapsburgs the most important ruling house in Europe.

Charles was afraid that other European powers, jealous of Hapsburg wealth and power, would try to seize some of these lands if a woman were to ascend the throne in Vienna. He was not even certain that all of the Austrian dominions would accept a woman ruler. So as early as 1718, little more than a year after the birth of Maria Theresa, Charles established a rule of succession which he called the Pragmatic Sanction. This provided that all the Austrian lands of the Hapsburgs would remain under one ruler, and it established a complicated order of succession to the throne: first Charles's own daughters, then the daughters of his older brother, Joseph. In the years between 1718 and his death in 1740, Charles was able to get all the Hapsburg kingdoms and principalities, and most of the major European powers, to accept the Pragmatic Sanction.

Thus, when Charles died, Maria Theresa was immediately recognized by most of Europe as the ruler of Austria. Furthermore, her husband, Duke Francis of Lorraine, was a logical candidate for election as emperor of the Holy Roman Empire. However, Charles Albert, Elector of Bavaria, had never recognized the Pragmatic Sanction. He was a descendant of a daughter of Emperor Ferdinand I, and thus claimed that he had as much right as Maria Theresa to the Austrian dominions. He also announced that he was a candidate for Emperor. There were also two other claimants to the Austrian lands: King Philip V of Spain and the Elector Augustus III of Saxony.

Prussian Invasion of Silesia

This dispute over the succession to the Austrian and imperial thrones seemed to Frederick to offer an opportunity to obtain additional strength and territories for Prussia. The Hohenzollerns had an ancient claim to the rich duchy of Silesia, just south of Prussia, which was owned by the Austrian Hapsburgs. Frederick wanted Silesia, and was not too concerned about the legality of his claim, although it was a real one. He simply believed that his army gave him the power to take Silesia, at a time when Austria was seriously troubled elsewhere. He was operating on the principle that might makes right.

Early in December, 1740, Frederick massed troops at the border of Silesia, under the command of Field Marshal Count Kurt von Schwerin. On December 11, Frederick sent word to Vienna that he would join Austria's alliance against Charles Albert, and vote for Francis to be emperor, if Austria would cede Silesia to Prussia. Knowing that the reply would be negative, on December 16 the young king ordered his troops into Silesia before there was time for an answer from Vienna.

The Prussians met with little resistance. Silesia had long been bled of its wealth to support other areas of the empire and the people felt no great loyalty to the Hapsburgs or to Austria. Also there were many Protestants, who flocked to welcome the advancing troops as deliverers from the enforced Catholicism of Austrian domination. The Prussians distributed pamphlets, "Proclamation to the Silesians," assuring the people of the invaders' goodwill. Frederick promised that his troops would keep order; he would see to it that army discipline was enforced in order that civilians could be secure in their possessions. Most of Silesia, except the strongly Catholic south, accepted the Prussians without opposition. Breslau opened its gates on January 3, without a struggle. As Frederick wrote home to a friend, only twenty men and two officers died in this campaign.

However, Austria and Maria Theresa had no intention of allowing Frederick to occupy Silesia and detach it permanently from the Austrian Empire. Furthermore, Austria, with ten times the population of Prussia, could turn its full attention to recovering the province. Although Charles Albert of Bavaria was challenging Maria Theresa's right to the Austrian throne, he would not risk war without the support of France or Britain, and they remained neutral.

While an Austrian army was slowly assembled in nearby Bohemia and on the Moravian-Silesian border, Hungarian raiders began to penetrate into Prussian-held Silesia. In March, 1741, Field Marshal Count William von Neipperg led an Austrian army of about 20,000 men across the snow-covered Sudeten mountain passes into Silesia. He advanced toward Ohlau, the main Prussian supply base in central Silesia.

Frederick, who was now commanding the Prussian forces in the field with Schwerin as his second-in-command, was completely surprised by this Austrian move. The Prussian army was scattered farther south and east in Silesia. The Austrians had cut Frederick's line of communications with central Silesia and with Berlin.

Encounter at Mollwitz

Hastily Frederick and Schwerin concentrated 22,000 men, then marched northward to seek the Austrians. The two armies, nearly equal in strength, cautiously probed toward each other. On April 7 there was a heavy spring snowstorm, which hindered operations, but early on April 10 the Prussians, marching northward from Oppeln, encountered the Austrian army, camped in and around the town of Mollwitz. It was late morning, and the Austrians were preparing their noon meal. A prompt Prussian attack probably would have overwhelmed the Austrians without a serious fight.

But this was Frederick's first battle. Instead of throwing his troops into Mollwitz, he ordered the army to deploy into a formal battle array. He fussed over details, and while his army was getting ready, the Austrians were also hastily forming up. By the time the Prussian army began to advance toward Mollwitz, with bands playing, it was the middle of the afternoon.

The Prussians were in two lines, with cavalry units and infantry battalions mixed together, on the theory that this was the best way that the horsemen and the foot soldiers could reinforce each other. The Prussian artillery, slightly in advance of the first line, unlimbered its guns when they were within range of the Austrian troops assembling near Mollwitz and opened fire. There was at first no response, since the Austrian artillery was not yet ready.

But the Austrian cavalry was ready. When the Prussian artillery fire became annoying, the Austrian horsemen charged. This charge had important results and affected Frederick's later cavalry tactics. We can best understand what occurred by reviewing the nature of European cavalry organization and tactics at that time.

Cavalry Organization and Doctrine

In the early years of the eighteenth century most European cavalry was heavily armed, slow, and cumbersome. There were two typical species: heavy cavalry and dragoons.

The heavy cavalryman usually wore a cuirass (or breastplate) and a helmet, and was armed with a carbine or with one or two pistols. Sometimes a heavy cavalryman would carry a carbine *and* a pistol or pistols. The traditional cavalry sword or saber was also carried, but it was an auxiliary weapon. Some armies had lancer units, but even the lancers usually carried firearms as well. In battle the cavalrymen relied upon firepower much more than they did upon shock. To permit more accurate fire they rarely charged at a rate of speed faster than a slow trot. The horses were large—they had to be to carry the weight of men, armor, weapons, and equipment—and slow. But this slowness did not matter with the kind of cavalry tactics in general use.

The dragoons were more lightly equipped men who did not wear armor, and who usually fought on foot, using their horses only as transportation. They were armed either with an infantry musket, or with a shorter-barreled weapon like the heavy cav-

At left, a hussar officer; middle, a cuirassier; right, a grenadier infantryman. (New York Public Library, Picture Collection)

alry carbine. The dragoons also carried swords or sabers, either on their belts or attached to the saddle, for use as an auxiliary weapon when they fought mounted instead of on foot. Their mounted tactics were exactly like those of the heavy cavalry: slow, ponderous, and based on firepower rather than on speed or shock.

The Austrians had developed a third type of cavalry called hussars. These were light horsemen, who had been found useful in Austria's centuries of conflict with Turkish light cavalry in Hungary and the Balkans. The hussars, who were usually Hungarians, were generally armed only with sabers, although there were some light lancer units as well. Their horses were light and fast. Hussars were excellent for scouting, and for screening before battle, and they were also effective in battle, both for shock action and to hit and run. In shock tactics, the hussars made up for their lack of weight and lack of firepower by their speed and momentum, and by their skill in handling their sabers and their horses.

All three types of cavalry were in the Austrian army at Mollwitz.

The Prussian army had both dragoons and heavy cavalry. There was little difference between these two types, save for the armor of the heavy cavalryman. Both were able to fight on horse and on foot, and in mounted action were carefully trained to fire in line, like the Prussian infantry.

Battle of Mollwitz—the Austrian Cavalry Charge

The Prussians were taken by surprise by the Austrian cavalry charge. But the steady Prussian infantry kept the attacking horsemen away from them by repeated volleys, so the Austrians naturally concentrated against the Prussian cavalry units. Since these were intermixed with the infantry battalions, this soon resulted in a number of wild cavalry melees, scattered all along the first Prussian line. Some of the surprised Prussian cavalry units were driven out of the line, and Austrian horsemen, led by hussars, poured through to repeat the process with the second Prussian line. By this time all of the Austrian heavy cavalry and dragoons had discharged their firearms, and were fighting like hussars with swords or—in a few cases—lances.

Soon the whole Prussian army was a scene of confusion. The artillery, which had been bypassed by the advancing Prussian infantry, now found itself also engaged by the Austrian horsemen. They fired in some confusion, doing almost as much damage to their own troops as to the attackers. The Prussian horsemen, having fired their weapons, were unable to cope either with the Austrian hussars or the hussarlike tactics of the remaining Austrian cavalry. Some Prussian cavalry units began to flee.

Frederick, inexperienced and confused, tried to do something to restore order in his shaken army. Courageously he dashed from one place to another, then began to try to gather a counterattack force of horsemen. By this time Field Marshal von Schwerin, seeing that the Prussian infantry battalions were still standing firm, felt that the battle could be saved, but he became concerned that the young king would be killed. Schwerin and other officers persuaded the king to leave the field, insisting that his presence would merely mean greater danger for all of his men. Schwerin promised that he would extricate the infantry from the battlefield.

Reluctantly, at about 4:00 P.M., the king accepted the insistent advice of his generals. Following some fleeing Prussian cavalry, he and a small escort galloped back to Oppeln. But when they arrived there, after dark, they discovered that the town had been seized by Austrian hussars. The king and his escort galloped away, and near midnight stopped to rest at the little town of Löwen, where there was a small Prussian garrison. The king was utterly dejected—all his dreams of glory were smashed. He had been defeated in his first battle, and his magnificent army was almost certainly destroyed.

As a matter of fact, his magnificent army was very much in existence.

Battle of Mollwitz—Prussian Infantry Attack

As soon as he had gotten Frederick safely off the field, Schwerin quickly restored a semblance of order to the Prussian battle line. Most of the cavalry had fled, but the splendidly trained infantry, even though most of the men were in their first battle, had held their positions, driving off every Austrian cavalry charge. Now, to the beat of drums, and in response to trumpet calls, the infantry closed up the gaps in their ranks, left by the disappearance of the cavalry. The exhausted Austrian horsemen, unable to prevent this realignment of the Prussian infantry, fell back to rejoin their own infantry, still near Mollwitz. By his failure to throw in his infantry after the initial success of his cavalry, Neipperg had lost his chance to win a decisive victory and to end the war.

Now, to their amazement, the Austrians saw the undefeated Prussian infantry advancing steadily toward them. The Prussian artillery had also stood its ground against the Austrian hussars. Now the guns were back in action, and had moved forward to support Schwerin's infantry attack.

This was too much for the Austrians. Before the Prussian infantry got close enough to fire a volley, the Austrian line began to crumble under the Prussian artillery fire. First to leave were the cavalry, who had done their best to destroy those rugged Prussian infantry units, and who knew they could do no more. When the Prussian infantry began to fire withering volleys into their ranks, the Austrian infantry waited no longer. Suddenly the entire Austrian army was in flight. Neipperg was unable to rally his men until they had reached Grottkau and the Neisse (Nysa) River.

The dead and wounded were by all accounts nearly equal, although there is not general agreement as to the numbers. Each side lost about 1,500 dead, about 3,000 wounded, and 1,000 missing or prisoners.

At two o'clock the following morning a messenger from Schwerin found Frederick, and reported the victory. Shortly after dawn Frederick, amazed but grateful, was riding over the battlefield. Three lessons of the battle were impressed upon his mind. First, he swore never to leave an undecided battle again and let others win it for him; he never forgave Schwerin for having sent him from the field. Second, he determined that he would not mix infantry and cavalry in the middle of a battle line. And third, he resolved to change Prussian cavalry organization and tactics completely.

The Prussian victory at Mollwitz amazed Europe, and increased the respect of other nations for Frederick and Prussia. Other German states that had been thinking of joining Austria now changed their minds. France sent an envoy—the leading French soldier, Marshal Duke Charles de Belle-Isle—to seek an alliance with Prussia against Austria and England. Elector Charles Albert of Bavaria, of course, was also prepared to join the alliance against Austria.

Belle-Isle arrived at Frederick's headquarters in a camp near Strehlen, in central Silesia. From there the king was directing two major efforts simultaneously. First, he was consolidating his control over all of Silesia north of the Neisse River. Second, he was in the process of reorganizing his cavalry and developing new cavalry doctrine.

While Belle-Isle observed approvingly, Frederick himself directed the siege and final assault on the fortress of Brieg, on the Oder River, east of Mollwitz. This was the last important Austrian foothold north of the Neisse, although Neipperg still held all of Upper Silesia.

Late in May, 1741, Frederick signed a secret treaty of alliance with France. As a result, the French prime minister, Cardinal Fleury, was able to line up France, Prussia, Bavaria, Spain, and Saxony against Austria, to begin the War of the Austrian Succession. The only major European nation which remained faithful to the Pragmatic Sanction was England. Although in alliance with Austria, however, the English were not certain that they should get too actively involved against the strong coalition.

During the summer, French troops assembled in Bavaria. Although France did not declare war, these troops joined the Bavarian army and then the combined force marched down the Danube to invade Austria. The allies occupied Linz with little trouble. By September they were within 30 miles of Vienna.

The Austrian situation was now desperate, since the only important army available to defend Vienna was that of Marshal Neipperg, still facing Frederick in Silesia. Frederick urged the allies to march against Vienna, because he was sure that Neipperg would then be recalled from Upper Silesia, which would enable him to overrun the entire province. But stout-hearted Maria Theresa had called all of the Austrian militia to arms; a Hungarian army was being raised to come to the assistance of Austria; she called Field Marshal Count Franz von Khevenhüller, who had been commanding Austrian troops in Italy, to return to the defense of the capital. And she left Neipperg to oppose Frederick in Silesia.

The Bavarians and French, aware of this Austrian activity, decided to advance no farther. They probably could have taken the Austrian capital, because the hastily raised Austrian troops were of poor quality. Realizing this, in fact, Maria Theresa had already decided to come to terms with Frederick so that she could deal more effectively with Bavaria and France.

On October 9, 1741, a secret meeting was held at the little town of Kleinschnellendorf, just south of the Neisse River in Silesia. There were three principal participants: Frederick, the British ambassador to Austria, and Field Marshal Neipperg of Austria. It was agreed that there would be a secret truce between Austria and Prussia, with Prussia retaining control of Silesia, as far as the Neisse River. The Austrian army was to be allowed to retire from Silesia to Moravia. The Prussians would pretend to pursue, and after a mock siege of two weeks, the fortress of Neisse would surrender to the Prussians.

Thus Frederick, by pretending to continue to fight, would not have to break his alliance with France. At the same time Maria Theresa would have Neipperg and his army available to deal with the Franco-Bavarian invaders of western Austria.

One of the provisions of this Agreement of Kleinschnellendorf was that it was to remain a secret; if either side were to disclose its terms, the agreement would automatically lapse. Thus it was as obvious to Maria Theresa as to Frederick that this was merely a temporary truce of convenience. Either side could break it at any time, simply by revealing the terms, or by revealing the mere fact that there had been an agreement.

For the moment, however, it was convenient to both sides to have the terms carried out exactly as agreed. After some mock skirmishing, the Austrians withdrew from Upper Silesia to Moravia, where Maria Theresa was mobilizing her forces for the defense of her throne. After occupying Neisse, Frederick returned to Berlin on November 11.

Austrian Recovery

Frederick's allies were quite unaware of the secret treaty. Expecting Prussian cooperation, a Franco-Bavarian army invaded Bohemia late in November and quickly occupied Prague, the capital. On December 19, Charles Albert of Bavaria was crowned King of Bohemia, in Prague. Then, flushed with triumph, he was elected Holy Roman Emperor Charles VII at Frankfort on January 24, 1742. He was crowned at Frankfort on February 12. But in the two and one-half weeks between the election and coronation of Charles Albert, the entire situation in central Europe and the empire had changed.

The diplomatic and internal measures which Maria Theresa had begun in September had, by early December, brought about the mobilization of more than 100,000 men for the protection of Vienna. These forces were formed into three major armies. Neipperg, in Moravia with one army, was responsible for keeping an eye on the Prussians, while he was at the same time ready to defend Vienna from any unexpected threat, and to act as a general reserve for the other two armies.

Khevenhüller, with the largest Austrian army, marched up the Danube, as the French and Bavarians hastily withdrew before him. On December 27 he reached Linz, still held by a

41

Franco-Bavarian garrison. After a siege of nearly a month, Linz surrendered. Khevenhüller at once marched into Bavaria. Thus, in late January, just as Charles Albert was being elected emperor, his lands were being invaded by Austrian troops. On Februrary 12, the day that Charles Albert was being crowned in Frankfort, his capital, Munich, was occupied by Khevenhüller.

The third Austrian army, under the command of Prince Charles of Lorraine—brother-in-law of Maria Theresa—marched north into Bohemia, to threaten the French and Bavarian troops holding Prague. At this time, in fact, the Bavarians were beginning to evacuate Bohemia, to return to the defense of their threatened homeland.

Then, suddenly, the entire military picture in Bohemia again changed dramatically, and the Austrians found themselves once more on the defensive.

Frederick Resumes the War

It is not clear whether Frederick or Maria Theresa first disclosed the terms of the Agreement of Kleinschnellendorf. Some historians believe that she did it in order to embarrass the Prussian king with his allies. She had clearly regained confidence, now that Austrian military strength had been restored. With the allies in flight in Upper Austria and Bavaria, she probably had come to the conclusion that Silesia could be retaken. Other historians, however, believe that Frederick falsely accused the Austrians of having failed to keep the secret of the agreement. He did it, they believe, so that he could join the Bavarians and French in the conquest of Bohemia, and prevent the Austrians from becoming so strong that they would be able to reconquer Silesia.

Whatever the truth may be, Prussian troops invaded Bohemia and Moravia in January, 1742. But planned cooperation with the Bavarians and French collapsed when the Bavarians withdrew. The French troops, under aged Marshal Count François de Broglie, were too weak and too short of supplies to leave the fortifications of Prague. This left Prince Charles of Lorraine free to turn his attention against Frederick and the Prussians.

During the next three months the Austrian and Prussian armies maneuvered warily in eastern Bohemia and northern Moravia. Snow and mud kept both sides from any serious efforts to engage in battle.

Frederick, from his headquarters in Olmütz, in Moravia, sent his cavalry raiding deep into Austria, reaching as far as the Danube and the outskirts of Vienna. But these diversions did not worry either Maria Theresa or Prince Charles of Lorraine. After the conquest of Bavaria, Khevenhüller sent reinforcements to the Austrian army in Bohemia. In April, Charles felt strong enough to carry the campaign more aggressively against Frederick. He moved to threaten Frederick's line of communication from Olmütz back into Silesia. At the same time Hungarian troops—mostly hussars and light infantry—began raiding into Silesia.

On April 25, Frederick evacuated Olmütz, and moved northwest into Bohemia, seeking to force Charles into battle. But Charles, informed of Frederick's movements by the friendly population, was able to avoid battle, while his hussars kept harassing the Prussian line of communication. Finally, in mid-May, when Frederick was camped near Kuttenberg, just south of the Upper Elbe, Charles received orders from Vienna to use his superior strength to fight a battle.

Slipping around Frederick, Charles placed his army on the Prussian line of communication and encamped at Czaslau and Ronnow on May 16. That night the Austrians set out, planning to attack the Prussians before dawn. But instead of being spread out in several camps, as the Austrians expected, Frederick's entire army was bivouacked at Chotusitz and organized for battle. Alert Prussian patrols and sentries fired on the Austrians as they approached, and Charles decided to wait for dawn. He found Frederick ready for battle.

About 8:00 A.M. the two armies faced each other, about 1,000 yards apart, both formed in two lines of infantry, with cavalry on either flank. There were about 30,000 Austrians, to 21,000 Prussians in the opposing battle lines. But Frederick had held out an additional force of about 7,000 men and 76 guns, hidden a few miles behind his right rear. He evidently planned to use this as an enveloping force if the opportunity offered.

The battle was opened by a Prussian cavalry charge on the

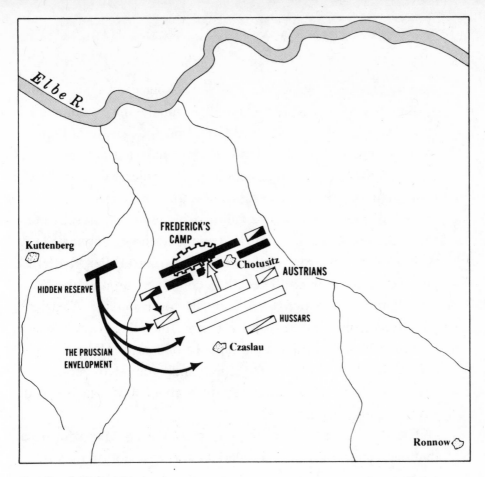

Battle of Chotusitz

Austrian left, but this was not followed up by the infantry because of clouds of dust the horses stirred up. The Austrians then
attacked the Prussian center, breaking through the first line
and advancing to Chotusitz and the Prussian camp, where they
were finally stopped by the Prussian second line in bloody

45

man-to-man fighting. There was a prolonged struggle in and around the town and the camp, but finally the outnumbered Prussian center fell back to re-form, and the Austrians set the town on fire. A no-man's-land of fire separated the opposing lines and prevented further action in the center, while the Austrians were plundering the Prussian camp.

At this point Frederick committed his hidden reserve, to envelop the Austrian left. These fresh battalions, supported by their artillery, overran a number of Austrian artillery batteries on Charles's left flank. They then continued around the Austrian flank, to threaten their rear. In confusion the Austrians withdrew from the field to Habern 15 miles away, where Charles was able to assemble only 15,000 men. His army had lost more than 3,000 men killed and wounded, and about 3,300 prisoners. Prussian losses were about 4,500 men killed, wounded, and missing.

The Prussian victory at Chotusitz convinced Maria Theresa that she could not defeat Frederick—at least not at that time. In order to be able to concentrate against France and Bavaria, she decided to conclude peace with Prussia, letting Frederick have Silesia. She hoped that there might be a later opportunity to regain the province, but that would have to wait.

On June 11, 1742, representatives of Austria and Prussia signed a peace treaty at Breslau. Austria gave up all except the southwestern corner of Silesia. The Treaty of Breslau was ratified at Berlin on July 28.

So ended the First Silesian War. But the War of the Austrian Succession, which had started as a result of Frederick's invasion of Silesia, continued. Austria now was able to turn full attention to the remaining allies opposing the Pragmatic Sanction—France and Bavaria were still holding the field in Bohemia and Germany, while Spain and Naples were threatening Austrian possessions in Italy.

CHAPTER 4

The Second Silesian War

Using the Peace

While the war continued in western and southern Germany, Frederick used the peace he had won to improve his armies, to rebuild the depleted treasury of Prussia, and to strengthen the defenses of Silesia. He realized that Maria Theresa still hoped to regain Silesia. So he wanted to be ready for war at any time. He continued to work on improving the cavalry; but he did not neglect the infantry. He gave generous money prizes for excellence in military contests of skill for soldiers and officers. He increased the strength of his standing army to 140,000 men. He began realistic peacetime maneuvers under actual warlike conditions. He started an informal school for his officers, to encourage them in improving their professional competence. This was the origin of Prussia's famous *Kriegs Akademie*, or War College.

Frederick wrote voluminously during these two years of peace. In addition to light correspondence he began a serious book: *History of My Time*. He also began to write down his ideas on military matters, intending to improve and refine these in future years. He built a new Berlin Opera House, and strengthened the Prussian Academy of Sciences. He took every opportunity to gain the confidence and goodwill of his subjects, encouraging them, whenever he was in Berlin, to come to him for settling disputes, or to obtain royal assistance in their private problems. Unlike his father, however, he did not force his attentions on the people. As a result, he soon had the loyalty of his subjects, including the Silesians.

Despite his youth, legends began to grow up around Frederick, who became a beloved and heroic figure to his people. They were pleased with his simple, plain clothing, and cheered him when he appeared quietly among them, without attendants. He made no pretense to be a man of the people; although always available to his subjects, he held himself aloof. His German was poor—he much preferred to speak French. But this did not bother the citizens. Nor did it bother his admiring soldiers, when he unexpectedly visited their messes and ate meals with them.

During this period of peace, Frederick arranged the marriage of his young cousin, Princess Sophie Augusta Frederica Catherine of Anhalt-Zerbst, to the Grand Duke Peter, nephew of Czarina Elizabeth of Russia. This obscure princess would later become famous as Catherine the Great.

Frederick kept a close watch on the progress of the War of the Austrian Succession. In 1742 the Austrians had driven the French and Bavarians out of Bohemia. The next year further Austrian and English victories brought them to the Rhine. Frederick believed that Austria's successes would give Maria Theresa confidence to try to regain Silesia. He was particularly concerned when England, Holland, Sardinia, and Saxony pledged themselves, at the Treaty of Worms, September 13, 1743, to recognize Austria's boundaries as they had been before the war. They ignored Prussia's claim to Silesia by the Treaty of Breslau. He decided that the best way to prevent Austria from retaking Silesia was to enter the war again on the other side.

Prussia Reenters the War

On June 5, 1744, Frederick negotiated the Treaty of Paris with France and with Emperor Charles VII—former Charles Albert of Bavaria. France agreed to a double invasion of Austria, and Frederick agreed to attack Bohemia. Bavaria would be returned to the emperor, and Frederick was to receive part of Bohemia. The combined invasion was to begin at the end of August.

Early in July, 1744, before the French were ready to start their part of the planned offensive, Prince Charles of Lorraine led an Austrian army of 70,000 men across the Rhine into the French provinces of Alsace and Lorraine. Frederick sent a message to Paris, assuring the French that he would relieve the pressure on them by moving two weeks earlier than he had planned.

On August 17 Frederick advanced with 80,000 men across the mountainous borders of Bohemia. About two-thirds of the army marched by way of Saxony—Frederick did not bother to get permission—while the rest went through Silesia. The two forces met at Prague. After a siege of only seven days, that city surrendered on September 16, 1744. In these operations Frederick lost only 40 men and captured a garrison of 12,000.

Bohemian Campaign

Frederick did not tarry at Prague. He had learned that his plan of helping the French had been successful. The Austrian army had recrossed the Rhine, and was marching to oppose him in Bohemia. Frederick, certain that the French and Bavarians would be following Charles, saw an opportunity to catch the Austrian army in a trap. He marched southeastward, to meet the Austrians near Vienna, only to learn a few days later that the French were still lingering on the Rhine.

Instead of having the Austrian army in a trap between the French and Prussian armies, it was now obvious to Frederick that he was in danger of being trapped himself. He was opposed by two Austrian armies—one already in Bohemia under Field Marshal Otto von Traun, the best of the Austrian generals, the other, under Charles, approaching from the west. Frederick returned to Prague to make new plans. The predominantly Catholic population of Bohemia was hostile to the Protestant Prussians, and there was little food for Frederick's troops or animals in the face of the onset of winter. Frederick tried in vain to lure Traun into a battle before Charles and his army arrived from the Rhine.

In the following weeks, the poorly supplied Prussian army

became ragged, hungry, and discouraged. During October and November about 17,000 men deserted. Early in November Prince Charles, reinforced by a Saxon contingent, approached Prague. Frederick, who now had less than 60,000 men, was unable to maneuver the 90,000 Austrians into a situation where he could fight on equal terms. Without adequate supplies, Frederick realized that he could no longer maintain himself in Bohemia. So, during November, 1744, the Prussians retreated to Silesia, where Frederick was able to resupply his troops.

On January 8, 1745, Austria, England, Holland, and Saxony concluded the Treaty of Warsaw, a Quadruple Alliance against Frederick. The objective of the allies was to regain Silesia for Austria, and to destroy Prussian power completely.

Frederick was in a desperate situation. He now knew he could not rely on the French. To raise money he melted down all of the silver he could get in Berlin—including the silver service of his royal palace. He also sold or melted down the palace furniture and all ornamental objects, including the chandeliers. He sent the Old Dessauer, Prince Leopold of Anhalt-Dessau who had helped his father build the Prussian army, to take command in Silesia. Frederick himself prepared his forces in Prussia for operations in the spring.

Silesian Campaign

The Austrians did not wait until spring, however. Maria Theresa ordered her armies to invade Silesia at the beginning of

February, thinking they would soon drive Frederick out of the province. The Old Dessauer, aching from rheumatism, and resting on a cart, directed the defense. He outmaneuvered the Austrians, and in three weeks drove them back across the Bohemian mountains. But Traun reorganized his army, and prepared to invade Silesia again in the spring.

Frederick returned to Silesia in March, determined to have a battle with the Austrians and win it, "or none of us shall see Berlin again." Then, in April, he learned that a Saxon army was marching northeastward toward Brandenburg from the Elbe, not only threatening his army's lines of communication, but also endangering Berlin.

Frederick sent directions for the defense of Berlin, ordering the garrison to evacuate the capital, if necessary. He knew that the Saxon move was merely a raid, and correctly guessed that it was an allied attempt to divert his attention from Silesia. He forgot Berlin, and concentrated on the more important matter of defeating the Austrians.

Meanwhile there had been a change in the Austrian command in Bohemia. In the preceding campaign Traun had been responsible for maneuvering Frederick out of Bohemia. But in the meantime French and Spanish armies had inflicted a series of defeats on the Austrian forces in Italy. Maria Theresa therefore sent Traun to take command in Italy, leaving Prince Charles of Lorraine in command in Bohemia. Charles was less skillful than Traun and more cautious. He timidly remained in Bohemia through April and much of May. Frederick, who was anxious for battle, had been expecting an Austrian invasion of Silesia. Now, because of this delay, he was thinking of going back into hostile Bohemia to seek battle. But the Prussian king was no less anxious than Maria Theresa. She ordered Charles to advance into Silesia at once. Reluctantly he began to move in late May.

As soon as Frederick was fairly certain that the Austrians were beginning to move, he put his own plan into effect. The purpose was to encourage Charles to continue the advance, and to lure the Austrians into a "mousetrap." Frederick pretended to spread his entire army all along the border, as though covering all of the possible mountain crossings from Bohemia along a front of 125 miles. Actually he was sure that Charles would head for Breslau, capital of Silesia, and so Frederick had most of his army—about 60,000 men—concentrated about midway between Breslau and Neisse. The troops were centrally located, so they could move quickly to block any Austrian advance.

During the first two days of June, 1745, the Austrians, about 80,000 strong, moved through the passes west of Landshut. On the night of June 1–2, Austrian hussars reconnoitered all along the Bohemian-Silesian frontier, and found that Prussian campfires were burning as usual. Then early on June 3 Charles received reports that these scattered Prussian detachments were retreating in confusion to the Oder.

Charles was now certain that he had caught Frederick napping. He therefore decided to plunge through the center of the widely scattered Prussian forces to reach Breslau; then he could defeat the Prussians in detail as they tried to concentrate. The Austrian army marched eastward from Landshut, and on the night of June 3 camped near Hohenfriedberg.

Actually, as soon as the Austrian-Saxon army had begun to appear in the passes, Frederick had quietly moved his army to the vicinity of Striegau. All during their march from Landshut to Hohenfriedberg, the Austrians had been carefully watched by hidden Prussians. A few detachments of Prussian troops, pretending to retreat hastily, had allowed themselves to be seen by the Austrians. While detailed reports of the enemy movement were sent to Frederick, these retreating decoys went about 5 miles and set up a dummy camp, where they lit campfires. Then, that night, following several parallel roads, the entire Prussian army marched silently toward the Austrian camp.

Battle of Hohenfriedberg

Just as dawn broke, about 4:00 A.M. on June 4, the Prussian troops swept forward. They quickly overwhelmed the Austrian outposts, and advanced into the camp. The Saxon contingent was completely destroyed shortly after 6:00 A.M. The Austrians, despite surprise, fought more stoutly. But the Prussian cavalry won the battle almost single-handed.

On the Prussian left, young Major General Hans Joachim von Ziethen led a charge across the Striegau River. The swampy riverbanks had been considered impassable by Charles, and Ziethen's horsemen completely routed the surprised Austrian left wing. At about the same time Austrian defensive fire briefly halted the Prussian infantry advance in the center. But Lieutenant General von Gessler, commanding the dragoons in the second Prussian line, led his horsemen through a gap in the enemy

Frederick inspecting prisoners after the Battle of Hohenfriedberg.
(*New York Public Library, Picture Collection*)

infantry line, then dashed on into the Austrian camp. These
two cavalry blows shattered the Austrians, who began to retreat. Frederick himself led another cavalry charge against an
Austrian artillery battery covering the retreat, and it became
a rout.

Among Prussian trophies were 76 colors, 66 cannon, and
nearly 6,000 prisoners. The Austrians and Saxons also lost 9,600
killed and wounded. Total Prussian losses were 900 dead and
3,800 wounded.

Frederick promptly pursued the Saxon and Austrian refugees
back into Bohemia. But he soon encountered the same diffi-

culties that had plagued him in the previous campaign. Because of the hostility of the Bohemian people, he was forced to detach substantial portions of his army to protect his line of communications as he advanced. By the time he had reached Charles's defensive positions, near Königgrätz, the Prussian army had dwindled to less than 30,000 men. Although the Austrian army was now little larger than his, it was strongly entrenched. Frederick did not wish to attack these fortifications, and so encamped west of the Elbe River at Chlumnetz.

Watchful Waiting

During the next three months the two armies faced each other across the Elbe. There were a number of skirmishes, but Frederick was unable to entice Charles into a battle in the open. Meanwhile the Austrian strength soon grew to more than 40,000 men, while Frederick's continued to dwindle.

There had, however, been a number of other developments elsewhere in Europe which encouraged Frederick to stay in his exposed position in Bohemia. On May 10, before the Battle of Hohenfriedberg, French Marshal Maurice de Saxe had decisively defeated a British-led allied army at Fontenoy, in Austrian Flanders. In the following weeks Saxe overran most of the Austrian Netherlands, which was a severe blow to both Austria and England.

The English, in fact, found this combination of defeats too discouraging. They knew that as long as Austria was fighting

Prussia the allies would not be able to concentrate sufficient force against Britain's main enemy: France. So the British government sought a formula which would bring about a negotiated peace between Prussia and Austria. They felt that the changed political situation in Germany might provide the formula.

In January, 1745, Emperor Charles VII had died, and his son Maximilian had made peace with Maria Theresa, announcing that he would not seek the imperial title for himself. Thus, before the spring and summer defeats had changed the political and military situation, Maria Theresa had hopes that her husband, Grand Duke Francis, might be elected the new emperor. The French and Prussian victories now made this doubtful.

The British hoped that Maria Theresa would be willing to recognize Prussian ownership of Silesia if, in return, Frederick —one of the nine electors—were to promise to vote for the election of Francis to be emperor. Frederick agreed, but to the surprise of both English and Prussians, Maria Theresa said that if it took Prussia to elect her husband emperor, she would have none of it. Furthermore, she is reputed to have said, "I would as soon part with my petticoats as with Silesia."

Nevertheless, Francis was elected on September 13, and Maria Theresa was overjoyed. The war in recent months had not been going as well as she had hoped, but at least two of her objectives had been attained. She was secure in her control of all Austrian territories except Silesia and the Netherlands, and she knew that her armies now had Frederick in a difficult situation in Bohemia.

Two weeks later Frederick decided that the time had come

for him to withdraw from Bohemia. His army was barely 22,000 strong. He knew that Prince Charles, who now had more than 40,000 men, had been ordered by Maria Theresa to bring him to battle. Outnumbered about two to one, and with his troops short of all kinds of supplies, the Prussian king did not care to risk battle.

Battle of Soor

Frederick marched north toward the passes between Trautenau and Landshut, closely followed by the Austrians. On the evening of September 29, 1745, the little Prussian army encamped in a valley near the village of Soor. Charles now used the tactics that Frederick had employed in the preliminaries to Hohenfriedberg.

During the night the Austrian army, preceded by a screen of hussars, silently marched through the woods to the east and north of the Prussians. The squeaking axles of the Austrian gun wheels were muffled with rags; every man obeyed strict orders to keep absolute silence. By dawn the Austrians were securely in position on heights to the Prussian right rear, covering Frederick's only line of retreat to Silesia. Expecting that the Prussians would withdraw southward, to seek another route for retreat, Charles had left an ambush force of about 12,000 men several miles to the south of the Prussian position. The Austrians were thus prepared for any move the Prussians might make.

Or so they thought.

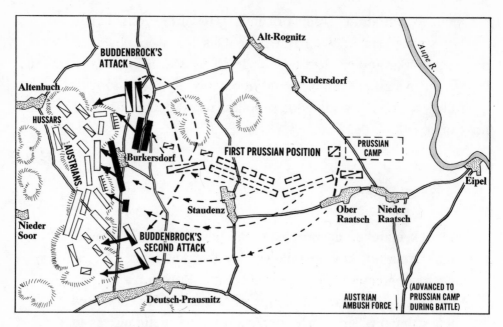

Battle of Soor

Actually, when the Austrian artillery opened fire from the heights on the Prussians in the valley near Soor, Frederick and his troops were already forming for battle. His alert patrols had reported the Austrian movement before dawn. Charles had outmaneuvered him, but had failed to surprise him. Frederick's army had been camped in line of battle, at right angles to the Austrians on the heights. He ordered his entire army to wheel to the right, under the eyes and the belching massed cannon of the Austrians on the heights.

The Prussian troops ignored the Austrian artillery, despite the gaps which it tore in their ranks. As though on the drill ground, they swung about, until the two lines faced each other, with the Prussian left flank almost opposite the right flank of the Austrian line on the hills, and the Prussian right opposite the Austrian center.

Suddenly every Prussian unit did a half-right face. They were placed by this unexpected maneuver in an oblique formation, with only the leading Prussian units opposite the Austrian left. To the right front of the infantry were the Prussian cuirassiers, under the command of General Heinrich Wilhelm von Buddenbrock. In accordance with Frederick's plan, Buddenbrock suddenly led his horsemen in an abrupt charge uphill. Closely behind him came the oblique column of Prussian infantry.

Heading for the waiting cavalry on the Austrian left, the Prussian horsemen ignored ragged carbine fire. They tore through the first line of Austrian horse, then into and through the second, and finally through a third line, which Charles had placed on his left to protect his artillery. The Austrian horsemen were scattered in confused flight, driven completely off the heights and into the woods in the rear. As they fled, the Prussian infantry stormed up the heights behind Buddenbrock's cavalry, to overrun and capture the cannon that Charles had massed on his left flank.

Buddenbrock wasted no time chasing the fleeing Austrian cavalry. He re-formed his men, turned back down into the valley, riding behind the infantry, and took position alongside the Prussian left flank cavalry. Now streaking to their left front, the entire cavalry force of the Prussian army headed up the slopes toward the Austrian right flank cavalry. The Austrian horsemen did not wait for them, but fled.

Again the Prussian cavalry did not bother to pursue. They simply changed front, swinging about to strike the exposed right flank of the Austrian infantry. At the same time the Prussian left flank infantry drove up the hill to attack from the front.

This ended the battle. By noon the entire Austrian army had fled. The Prussians had lost about 1,000 dead, 2,700 wounded, and 300 missing. The Austrians had lost about 4,500 dead and wounded, and more than 3,000 were captured. The Prussians also captured 22 cannon and 12 flags.

Meanwhile, the Austrian ambushing force had heard the noise of battle and had moved up behind the Prussians, overrunning their baggage train. They were looting the wagons when Frederick's victorious troops returned from the heights to drive them off. However, the Prussians lost most of their baggage, a severe hardship. All of Frederick's personal possessions were taken: his books, his flute, a collection of snuffboxes, and his favorite dog. (The dog was later returned.) The entire Prussian war chest was also lost. But the Prussian army held the field and their line of retreat was secure.

Frederick and his army stayed calmly for five days at the scene of their victory, foraging for food over the nearby countryside. Then they marched in a leisurely fashion over the passes and back into Silesia. They encountered no further Austrian opposition.

Winter Campaign

Frederick put his army into winter quarters near Liegnitz, then went on to Berlin. He hoped Maria Theresa would now make peace. But very soon he learned that Saxony and Austria were planning a winter campaign; two armies were to invade Brandenburg to destroy him. Prince Charles was to march from northern Bohemia toward Berlin, converging with another Austrian-Saxon army under Count Rutowsky, advancing from western Saxony. Furthermore, there was a danger that Russia would also enter the war, and invade Prussia from the east.

Frederick immediately rejoined his army at Liegnitz. He ordered Prince Leopold, the Old Dessauer, commanding an army of 30,000 men based at Halle, to advance southeastward, up the Elbe River, and to meet him near Dresden.

Frederick, who now had about 40,000 men, marched westward, intercepting Charles's army near Hennersdorf and Görlitz on November 23 and 24, 1745. In a confused, but not very hard-fought, two-day battle Frederick drove Charles back into Bohemia after capturing 5,000 prisoners.

Battle of Kesselsdorf

Frederick then discovered that Prince Leopold had hardly moved at all. However, after Frederick sent some sharply worded rebukes to his father's old campanion, the insulted prince began to advance. He occupied Meissen (near Dresden) on December 12, then continued on, seeking a battle.

On December 14 Leopold found Rutowsky and his army of 35,000 troops waiting in a strongly entrenched position on a hill near the village of Kesselsdorf. The Austrian-Saxon army held a formidable defensive position, four miles long, on a rocky hill. The icy slopes were covered with well-emplaced cannon. Leopold, usually a calm and cautious man, was so enraged by the messages he had been receiving from Frederick that he decided to attack, despite the enemy's numerical superiority and favorable defensive position.

At 3:00 P.M. Leopold formed up the Prussian infantry opposite the allied center. He spread his cavalry out toward both flanks to cover the entire enemy front. He placed himself at the head of five infantry battalions which were to spearhead the attack of his right wing, near Kesselsdorf.

Before Leopold ordered the attack, the pious old soldier is said to have uttered the following prayer: "Lord God help me. . . . At least don't help those scoundrels, the enemy." Then, facing his troops, he waved his hat and cried: "In the name of Jesus, march!"

Up the icy slope the Prussians marched, those beautiful grenadiers that Leopold had trained so devotedly, slipping and sliding, their ranks torn by enemy artillery fire, but never faltering. They reached the top of the hill, but the first wave was beaten back by overwhelming numbers and firepower. Grimly the Old Dessauer re-formed them, then led them up again. The troops and their general stumbled over the bodies of dead comrades, but refused to admit a defeat which now seemed certain.

Suddenly an Austrian contingent on the hilltop cried "Victory!" and broke away from the line of defense to charge down the hill on the struggling Prussian infantry below. Leopold calmly threw in his cavalry at this moment, smashing the Austrian counterattack. Then he again led his infantrymen doggedly up the slope.

Meanwhile, in the center, Prince Maurice, Leopold's youngest son, had been more successful. Like his father, he led the advance himself. He and his men had waded through a moat, waist-deep in icy mud, and then clambered up to seize a foothold at the top of the cliff. There they clung, driving off Saxon counterattacks.

This success in the center, combined with the grim determinations of Leopold and his grenadiers on the right, was now too much for the Saxons. They wavered, and this gave Leopold and his men a chance to reach the top. Suddenly the entire allied line crumbled. As they retreated, the Prussian cavalry pursued.

The battle was over at 5:00 P.M. with a count of 3,800 enemy dead and wounded, and 6,700 prisoners. Prussian casualties were about 5,000. Leopold had three bullet holes in his coat.

Peace of Dresden

Frederick's army quickly overran Saxony. He left the Queen of Saxony with her young children in possession of the palace at Dresden, and made certain that his troops treated the Saxon population with kindness and courtesy. But he established firm control over the tiny nation.

The defeats at Soor, Hennersdorf-Görlitz, and Kesselsdorf convinced Maria Theresa that she should make peace. The Treaty of Dresden, signed on Christmas Day, 1745, ended the Second Silesian War. Austria ratified the earlier treaties of Breslau and Berlin, recognizing Prussian control of Silesia. Frederick received reparations of 1,000,000 thalers (12.5 million dollars) from Saxony. He recognized Francis as emperor.

The peace completed, Frederick returned to Berlin. Here, for the first time in his life, he was given a heartfelt demonstration of respect and love by his people. Forgotten were the hardships and costs of the war. The Berliners poured from the city to meet their king; they threw flowers and flocked about his carriage, cheering wildly.

Frederick was now admired not only by his own people, but by most Germans, as the new champion of the small German states. He was looked at by them as the heroic little man who had managed to win against the great power bullies. Many superstitious Germans had decided that he was bulletproof, since he had so often been exposed to death without having been scratched. It was also obvious to everyone in Europe that he was a military genius. From this time on he was called Frederick the Great.

CHAPTER 5

Uneasy Peace (1745–1755)

The Philosopher of Sans Souci

Frederick did not share the commonly held view that he led a charmed existence and was immune to death. Although he was only thirty-three, he prepared his affairs and those of the kingdom in anticipation of an early death. He had a tomb constructed in his vineyards, near Potsdam. His brother, Augustus William, was appointed his successor and called the Prince of Prussia. And the army was kept ready for instant campaigning.

Otherwise Frederick showed little concern for what might happen, or who might rule after him. He remarked, with his usual cynicism, that thrones did not long remain vacant. The future kings of Prussia, he said, "can do as they like. . . . I have acquired Silesia—it is up to my successors to keep it."

Opposite his waiting tomb Frederick constructed a comfortable, medium-sized house which he named *Sans Souci* ("without care"). He furnished it with furniture, drapes, and ornaments from Paris. After May of 1747, when the house was completed, he paid little attention to his palaces in Berlin and Potsdam. At Sans Souci he collected friends to share his leisure

Frederick playing the flute at Sans Souci.

hours. In the company of these friends—mostly French—he cultivated the arts, music, and literature. He never allowed any mention of his administrative or ceremonial responsibilities while he was at Sans Souci in the evenings or on holidays.

In his leisure time Frederick shunned the Prussian soldiers and administrators on whom he relied in business hours in the conduct of the affairs of state. He considered that most of these men were crude and insensitive. Despite his passionate devotion to his people, and to the responsibilities of ruling Prussia, he still spoke German with a French accent.

One of the few military men among Frederick's close friends was a Scottish nobleman, James Edward Keith. This Jacobite refugee (no direct relation to Frederick's friends the von Keiths) had served with distinction in the Russian army, but offered his services to Prussia in 1747. Frederick accepted at once, promoted Keith to field marshal, and frequently invited him to Sans Souci.

Frederick never invited women to San Souci, and appears to have had little or no interest in female companionship. He hated his wife and rarely saw her.

Frederick's method of relaxation was to play the flute, compose music, and write. He wrote verses, plays, and letters, and continued his *History* and his military writings. Each day before dinner at Sans Souci there was a concert, with Frederick playing the flute. Voltaire came to live with him during the years from 1750 to 1753. Then he and Frederick quarreled, and Voltaire was sent from Prussia.

No one in Europe could understand this complicated, witty, brilliant, but peculiar man. Many of his fellow monarchs thought Frederick was insane. By the time he was forty years old, he was an international legend.

Administration of Prussia

Despite his insistence upon pleasure and relaxation, Frederick's capacity for administrative work was incredible. He extended his personal attention to every detail of everything in all of Prussia. He delegated nothing that he could handle himself, including daily audiences with his subjects on any matters that they might wish to discuss with him. His day was very full, from 3:00 A.M., when he arose, until he relaxed over a late dinner.

No other European monarch worked so hard and Frederick took great pride in his industrious activity, claiming that idleness was a form of death. He said that he owed service to his people, and that it was up to him to learn to enjoy his duties. Without a family or close associates, during daytime hours he poured his energies into the administration of his country.

Frederick continued his father's sound economic policies. He supported agriculture, but also encouraged the industrialization of Berlin, and built up the silk industry. He encouraged immigrants to settle the underdeveloped areas of Prussia and made regular tours to examine the state of manufacturing and agriculture. No gold or silver could leave Prussia. Like Frederick William before him, Frederick converted these precious metals into palace ornaments, so that they could be melted down later if necessary in order to pay his armies in the event of war.

Because of his close personal supervision, Frederick's administration had less corruption than that of any nation in Europe. His rule was also much less oppressive than that of his father. Although he was autocratic and dictatorial, and while he followed a system of justice which would be considered barbarous today, Frederick was far in advance of his times in humanitarian ideas. This aspect of his character doubtless came from his own mistreatment and cruel punishment at his father's hands. As a result, life for even his most helpless subjects was far more humane than in any other kingdom of Europe.

The Prussian Army

Potsdam, with its barracks and drill fields, was quite near Sans Souci. Early every morning Frederick rode from his house of culture and immersed himself in the business of soldiering and governing. He devoted constant attention throughout the interval of peace to building up the Prussian army. He knew that Maria Theresa would try to regain Silesia if she had the opportunity. He believed that the peace was just a breathing spell.

Frederick continued to give instruction to his officers and instituted regular courses of study for them. He increased the size of the army and channeled all available funds into his war chest. His goal was 180,000 well-trained men. He set aside 20,000,000 thalers for military needs should Prussia go to war again.

Except for the cavalry, Frederick accepted his father's organization of the army, adding only some special staff departments under the General Directory, or War Ministry. But he recognized the tactical weaknesses of eighteenth-century armies, including his own: slowness, ponderousness, lack of imagination, slow rates of fire. He complained, for instance, that "our modern formations for combat, for the most part, are defective because they are all cast in the same mold: the infantry is in the center and the cavalry on the wings." While he did not make the kind of changes in methods of warfare that Gustavus Adolphus had done before him, or that Napoleon was destined to make after him, Frederick, with all of the objectivity that he urged upon his generals, sought ways to offset these defects in his own army, and to take advantage of them in an enemy army.

So Frederick became a conservative innovator. He found ways to increase speed and rapidity of fire, and made his officers think always in terms of mobility. By increasing his infantry's speed and the rate of fire of its muskets, he roughly doubled the effectiveness of his foot troops. By speed and agility, he realized, he could concentrate superior power at a critical point before a more ponderous foe could react effectively. He achieved his mobility and speed by reemphasizing and refining the drill and disciplinary methods inherited from his father.

The already rigid military discipline of the early eighteenth century became even more strict. Although Frederick was kind and considerate of his men, he insisted upon incessant, brutal, rigid drill discipline. The individual Prussian soldier was like a robot. Prussian units could change direction or front simultaneously or by small groups in succession; they could shift quickly into battle formation from marching column or vice versa, even over broken and irregular terrain.

The net result was infantry of high mobility, completely responsive to the will of the commander. Battalions could be shifted and massed at will on the battlefield to produce the maximum effect of fire and shock action at a chosen spot. Frederick, remembering the effectiveness of his maneuver at Soor, was particularly partial to oblique formations. In this way he could advance to combat against a much larger foe, without exposing his flank to envelopment. Frederick apparently took the idea from the ancient Theban and Macedonian armies, but its successful operation in eighteenth-century warfare depended upon perfect Prussian discipline.

Improvement of the Cavalry

Frederick probably devoted more attention to improving the effectiveness of his cavalry than he did to any other military matter. He recognized that this was one aspect of military affairs which his father had neglected.

Frederick forbade the use of firearms by the cavalry in mounted action—although his dragoons were trained to use carbines effectively in fighting on foot. But for mounted combat Frederick insisted that his horsemen rely entirely on speed, discipline, and shock action. They were to employ only the saber in the charge, disregarding any use of firearms against them by hostile cavalry and infantry.

Frederick had begun this change in cavalry tactics immediately after the Battle of Mollwitz. Now he made speed and shock action the cardinal points in his cavalry doctrine. He reduced the depth of the cavalry formation first to three ranks, then to two. With the individual troopers riding boot-to-boot, entire squadrons were trained to charge at a full gallop, across all kinds of terrain, keeping a perfect alignment. Like the infantry, cavalry units could change front rapidly, without losing their perfect formations. To preserve complete freedom of action and unlimited mobility for his cavalry squadrons, Frederick never interspersed them with infantry units after the fiasco of Mollwitz.

Frederick described his concept in the following words:

> As for cavalry attack, I have considered it necessary to make it so fast and so close for more than one reason: (1) so that this large movement will carry the coward along with the brave man; (2) so that the cavalryman will not have time to reflect; (3) so that the power of our big horses and their speed will certainly overthrow whatever tries to resist them; and (4) to deprive the simple cavalryman of any influence in the decision of such a big affair.
>
> So long as the line is contiguous and the squadrons well closed, . . . the enemy, being more open than we are and having more intervals, is unable to resist our shock. The force of our shock is double theirs, because they have many flanks and we have only one which the general protects to the extent possible, and finally because the fury of our attack disconcerts them. If they fire they will take to flight; if they attack at a slow trot, they are overthrown; if they wish to come at us with the same speed with which we attack, they come in confusion and we defeat them . . . in detail.

The individual troopers were painstakingly schooled in the details of tactics and techniques. Each man became a splendid horseman. All were required to practice unceasingly in the use of the saber, both offensively and defensively, while riding at full gallop. Day after day, under the king's critical but approving eye, the cavalry was put through its paces on the Potsdam parade ground. He took great pains with every detail—a rider's seat, the execution of a maneuver, the condition of weapons, horses, and equipment. There were frequent competitions, with money, sabers, and horses as prizes.

Development of Horse Artillery

Frederick realized that his insistence upon the use of the saber, and his refusal to permit his horsemen to use firearms, put them at a disadvantage in some instances. He understood the value of combining firepower and mobility. But he was convinced that the traditional method of doing this, by putting firearms in the hands of cavalrymen, was a mistake, resulting in unnecessary loss of mobility. So he decided to find some other way to give his cavalry firepower—to protect them in the defense and to support them in the attack.

His solution to this problem was perhaps the most important single organizational contribution which Frederick made to the warfare of his times. He created horse artillery. Horse-*drawn* field artillery had been in use since the time of Gustavus Adolphus, but the mobility of normal horse-drawn artillery was not equal to the demands of keeping up with Frederick's hard-riding, fast-moving cavalrymen. Frederick's horse artillery, on the other hand, was designed to move almost as rapidly. The guns were light howitzers. The cannoneers did not ride on the weapons, or on the ammunition-carrying caissons, as was done in the horse-drawn artillery. Instead, each gunner had his own

75

horse, reducing the load for the gun teams, and giving additional speed and flexibility.

There were two advantages in using howitzers. First, because these weapons fired at a shorter range, and with a smaller powder charge than the normal cannon, the walls of the tube could be lighter, thus reducing the overall weight of the weapon. Also, because of the higher, arching trajectory which the cannonball followed in its flight, the howitzer could be placed behind a hill for protection and could fire over the tops of hills or fortifications. Its shots would land on enemy troops on the other side, instead of whistling harmlessly overhead, as was often the case with the standard, flat-trajectory fieldpiece.

The highly trained horse artillery units could move almost as fast as the Prussian cavalry, and could go over ground impassable to other artillery. Frederick now had fire and movement at high speed.

Military Instructions for the Generals

During these years of peace this industrious and thoughtful man devoted much of his evening time to putting his ideas on military affairs in writing. By 1747 he had completed the first drafts of two books which summarized all of his thinking about the art of war. These were both continuously revised during the following eight years of peace.

One of these works was a general military handbook which Frederick called *Military Institutions*. This was a very comprehensive textbook on military organization, small unit tactics, and techniques, and a complete checklist of the duties of minor officers under various kinds of combat situations.

Far more important, however, was a work which Frederick first called *Military Instructions*, and later, in a revised edition, entitled *General Principles on War*. The document is most commonly known to history, however, as *The Instruction of Frederick the Great for His Generals*. In this, Frederick outlined in detail his observations on the art of warfare, discussed the military problems of Prussia as he saw them in 1747 (and later, in revised editions), and laid out the principal elements of what he called his "system" or "method."

At first Frederick showed his work to no one except his younger brother, Prince Augustus William, his successor to the throne. The king was afraid that if copies of this work were widely distributed, it would tell his potential enemies too much about his thinking, and about his specific strategic plans for the defense of Prussia against every possible threat. Evidently he also showed the manuscript to Field Marshal von Schwerin and one or two others of his most trusted military subordinates. Finally, in 1753, he had fifty copies of the book secretly printed and distributed to his senior generals and to the most promising younger officers of the army. Each officer receiving the book, carefully sealed, was required to take an oath that he would guard the book carefully, would never take it with him into the field in wartime, and would make arrangements so that in the event of his death the book, well sealed, would be returned to the king in person.

It is almost unbelievable that this thirty-five-year-old king could have foreseen almost all of the possible military situations which might face him in the defense of his country. Yet his estimates of the possible ways in which Prussia could be threatened proved to be complete, thorough, and accurate. His discussion of the ways in which these threats could be countered describes what he actually did during the Seven Years' War. One of the roughly sketched diagrams, which he probably drew in 1747, is almost an exact diagram of his plan for the Battle of Leuthen, which he fought in 1757. The concept for the Battle of Torgau is described in the section on "the Attack and Defense of Fortified Places." Similarly, the strategic plans for the invasion of Bohemia and Moravia described in the book, and for the defense of Silesia, Brandenburg, and East Prussia, were actually performed years later almost exactly as he foresaw.

In many respects this book, with its philosophical discussion of warfare and military theory, as well as its specific strategic plans, was truly the beginning of the Prussian analytical system of warfare, which was to make Prussia, and later Germany, the leading military nation of Europe for the better part of two centuries. The book also reveals much about the innermost thoughts of this witty, brilliant, and strange man, who was able to hide his thoughts so well from all those around him. With amazing candor he described some of his mistakes in the First and Second Silesian Wars, and showed how these mistakes should be avoided in the future. There are also some indications of reasons for the few mistakes which he made in the Seven Years' War, which would otherwise not be fully understandable.

In his *Instructions* Frederick reveals his complete mastery of those basic concepts of warfare that were later called "Principles of War," as well as his thorough understanding of the essential elements of military leadership.* A few extracts will tell us much about Frederick, about his army, and about his system of war.**

> The discipline and the organization of Prussian troops demand more care and more application from those who command them than is demanded from a general in any other service. . . . Our regiments are composed half of citizens and half of mercenaries. The latter, not attached to the state by any bonds of interest, become deserters at the first occasion. . . .

The king then went on to describe the various ways in which desertion could be prevented.

No general has ever been more proud of his army. Yet his assessment was objective:

> The greatest force of the Prussian army resides in their wonderful regularity, which long custom has made a habit, in exact obedience, and in the bravery of the troops. The discipline of these troops . . . has such effect that, in the greatest confusion of an action and the most evident perils, their disorder is still more orderly than the good order of their enemies. Consequently, small confusions are

* See Appendix for a summary of modern concepts of the "Principles of War" and of military leadership.

** All quotes are taken from the translation by Brigadier General T.R. Phillips in his book *Roots of Strategy,* with some minor modifications.

79

redressed in a moment and all evolutions are made promptly. A general of other troops could be surprised in circumstances in which he would not be if commanding Prussians, since he will find resources in the speed with which they form and maneuver in the presence of the enemy.

"As for Prussian infantry," he wrote, "it is superior to all rules. The power of the Prussians is in the attack. . . . I am of the opinion that the Prussians, with a resolute man at their head, could easily set right a [disaster], especially if the general has conserved the resources of the reserves." In those lines we have the secret of his later victories of Zorndorff and Torgau —and also of the disasters at Kunersdorf and Hochkirch, when even his own indomitable resolution could not retrieve disaster. This last quotation is only one of many in which Frederick stresses the importance of "the Principle of the Offensive." Time after time in the *Instructions* he reaffirms his conviction that the best defense is a strong offense.

In general the first of two opposing commanders who adopts an offensive attitude always reduces his rival to the defensive and makes him regulate himself on the movement of the attacker. . . .

I have already said, and I repeat it, that I would never put myself in an entrenchment, at least unless a terrible misfortune, such as the loss of a battle or a triple superiority on the part of an enemy forced me to do it. . . .

I have often said that for Prussians I would choose only unassailable [defensive] positions or else I would not occupy them at all, for we have too many advantages in attacking to deprive ourselves of them gratuitously. But . . . it is necessary to speak of this subject.

Following this last quotation, Frederick went on to say that once the enemy attacks the defensive position, the defender should "confound him with your cannon and then march straight at him to attack." Thus, even where circumstances forced him to the defensive strategically, Frederick urged the use of the offensive tactically.

Frederick was perhaps the first general of history to understand, and describe, the concept of a deep and mobile defensive formation, particularly in the defense of river lines. Then, once the enemy has committed himself to a line of advance, or to starting to cross the river, the centrally located mobile reserve should be thrown against the spearhead, since "your duty is to attack the enemy then."

In order to be able to apply the Offensive successfully, Frederick urged his generals to have superior combat power at the most decisive points on the battlefield. This superiority was to be achieved not only through the higher quality of the Prussian soldiery, but also by concentrating the maximum number of troops at places where the enemy was most vulnerable. No modern text on military doctrine can better summarize the interrelationship between the Principles of the Offensive Mass, Maneuver, Objective, and Economy of Force than one brief quotation from the *Instructions*:

All weak armies attacking stronger ones should use the oblique order. . . . The whole wing which is not fighting acts as a reserve for you. . . . I approve all methods of attacking provided they are directed at the point where the enemy's army is weakest and where the terrain favors them least.

This is only one of a number of instances in which Frederick wrote of the importance of making the best use of terrain—and, he added, to make good use of ground, "the first point is to know the locality well." He repeatedly told his generals to look over all the possible areas of combat and suggested ways in which they could make the best use of the terrain. "Knowledge of the country," he said, "is to a general what a rifle is to an infantryman and what the rules of arithmetic are to a geometrician. . . . Therefore study the country where you are going to act!"

Not only should a general know the ground on which he will have to fight, Frederick pointed out, but he should know as much as possible about the enemy with whom he will contest the control of that ground. "A great advantage is to be drawn from knowledge of your adversary, and when you know his intelligence and character you can use it to play on his weaknesses."

He then continued: "A general in all his projects should not think so much about what he wishes to do as about what his enemy will do; . . . he should never underestimate this enemy, but should put himself in his place to appreciate difficulties and hindrances the enemy could interpose; . . . he will be deranged at the slightest event if he has not foreseen everything and if he has not invented the means to surmount the obstacles." If, however, this careful planning has been adequate, Frederick continued, the general should not then overestimate his enemy. "It is essential to be objective and it is dangerous to delude oneself. . . . Put yourself in the place of your enemy, and all of the hindrances which you will have imagined and which he will not make for you, when war comes, will be just so many things that will facilitate your operations."

Napoleon frequently quoted and paraphrased Frederick's brilliant summation of the Principle of the Objective: "There is an ancient rule of warfare that cannot be repeated often enough: hold your forces together, make no detachments, and, when you want to fight the enemy, reassemble all your forces. . . . Petty geniuses attempt to hold everything; wise men hold fast to the most important resort. . . . He who would preserve everything preserves nothing."

Frederick stressed the importance of supply and logistical planning. "Understand that the foundation of an army is the belly. It is necessary to procure nourishment for the soldier wherever you assemble him and wherever you wish to conduct him. This is the primary duty of a general." He then went on to discuss the various problems of supplying an army, even to providing hand mills so that each company could grind its own flour, "because wheat can be found everywhere and the soldiers can grind it."

Frederick emphasized and reemphasized the need for a general to keep close and constant supervision over all of the actions of his officers and men. The general "should be more than an industrious, active, and indefatigable man; he should not forget one thing to execute another; and above all he should not despise those sorts of little details which pertain to vague projects. . . . Thus be vigilant and indefatigable, and do not believe, having made one tour of your camp, that you have seen everything."

There has probably never been a more practical leadership manual than Frederick's *Instructions*. He wrote: "The commander should practice kindness and severity, should appear friendly to the soldiers, speak to them on the march, visit them while they are cooking, ask them if they are well cared for, and alleviate their needs if they have any. Officers without experience in war should be treated kindly. Their good actions should be praised. Small requests should be granted them, and they should not be treated in an overbearing manner, but severity is maintained about everything regarding the service. . ."

"If you wish to be loved by your soldiers," he added, "husband their blood and do not lead them to slaughter." He cautioned, however, against false efforts to spare losses by timidity, which could in fact lead to even greater losses. "When you seem to be most prodigal of the soldier's blood, you spare it, however, by supporting your attacks well and by pushing them with the greatest vigor to deprive time of the means of augmenting your losses."

Frederick fancied himself as the "Philosopher-King" as well as the "Soldier-King." These two aspects of his nature are revealed in one prophetic passage:

When a general conducts himself with all prudence, he

can still suffer ill fortune; for how many things do not cooperate at all with his labors! Weather, harvest, the officers, the health or sickness of his troops, blunders, the death of an officer on whom he counts, discouragement of the troops, exposure of your spies, negligence of the officers who should reconnoiter the enemy, and finally betrayal.

All of these things were to happen to Frederick at one time or another, to undo his work, or to threaten him with disaster, or to cause a defeat. Yet, no matter what happened, he never forgot his own inspiring words: "Do not despair of winning, but do not expect any other success than that gained by your skill."

To the historian and to the biographer, however, perhaps the most important passages in the *Instructions* are those in which he stressed the need for a general to hide his personal feelings and thoughts, so that his enemies will not be able to guess his plans, and so that he will not worry his own troops by any indication of doubt or discouragement.

It is necessary to hide your secret intentions with the most specious pretexts that you are able to invent. . . .

The dissimulation of the general consists of the important part of hiding his thoughts. . . . While never despising his enemy in the bottom of his heart, he should never speak of him except with scorn. . . .

You must [in some cases] deceive your own officers and pretend to have designs which you want the enemy to attribute to you. He will be notified by the indiscretions of your officers, and your real intention will remain hidden.

85

Thus Frederick, in his own words, confirms what the historian suspects: He always wore a mask, deliberately made impenetrable even to his closest friends and associates. Only in his secret, closely guarded *Instructions* did the king let down the mask, and reveal his innermost thoughts as they really were. One of the most important messages he gave us in those frank comments is that everything else that he said or did or wrote was done with the intent to hide his thoughts, his aspirations, his very nature, from all of the world.

Selecting Offensive-Minded Generals

In his *Instructions* Frederick wrote: "My system is based on the idea that it is up to the infantry to expel the enemy and to push him, so to speak, off the field of battle, and that it is the cavalry which crowns the action." But this system also required, he knew, bold, vigorous, quick-thinking leaders. And, as he wrote somewhat sadly in his *Instructions*: "Offensive generals are rare among us; I know only a few. Nevertheless, it is only to these that [independent command] can be entrusted."

His particular problem was to find cavalry generals who would have the boldness and vigor to use that instrument of war, as he had developed it, in the manner which his system demanded. Most of the traditional cavalrymen of his and other armies were appalled by the idea of discarding firearms. Even the Austrians, from whom he had gotten the idea, thought that only hussars, who rarely were involved in a full-scale cavalry battle, should be without a gun of some sort.

But Frederick was soon able to develop cavalry leaders who understood his ideas, and who could carry them out perfectly. Outstanding among these were two men: Generals Friederich Wilhelm von Seydlitz, and Hans von Ziethen. Ziethen had been largely responsible for the victory at Hohenfriedberg, and in time became perhaps the best known of Frederick's generals. But Seydlitz was perhaps an even greater cavalry general. A foreign observer* at one of Frederick's annual maneuvers wrote about an incident which he observed, which perhaps best reveals Seydlitz's nature as well as his ability.

Seydlitz . . . was so skilful, so vigorous a horseman, that he could not conceive how an officer of cavalry could be made prisoner if his horse was not killed. Once he expressed this opinion while escorting the King. . . . Frederick, whom nothing escaped, was struck with his remarks, and decided to put him to the proof. The opportunity soon presented itself.

The escort was obliged to pass over a bridge; the king stopped in the middle of it, and turning toward Seydlitz, who was surrounded in front and rear, said to him:

"You pretend, Monsieur Seydlitz, that an officer of cavalry ought never to be made prisoner. Certainly that is the idea of a brave man; nevertheless there are occasions when one could surrender without dishonor. Suppose,

* Count de Rochfort, reported in *Idées Pratiques sur la Cavalerie*, as translated in Denison's *History of Cavalry*.

for instance, that we were enemies; you would not attempt to pass by force. What would you do then?"

Seydlitz, prompt as thought, drove in his spurs and threw himself with his horse into the torrent, and without suffering any injury, returned to the retinue near the king, whom he saluted, saying, "Sire, behold my reply."

Presumably the Count de Rochfort observed this incident in person. There were no foreign observers allowed, however, at the twelve-day maneuvers which Frederick held near Spandau, in the fall of 1755. War clouds were again gathering in Europe, and Frederick wished to be absolutely certain that his 150,000-man regular army was prepared for combat. And he wanted to be certain that his generals understood his *Instructions*. When the maneuvers were over, he was satisfied. His troops were in good condition; morale was excellent; training and discipline were perfect. Frederick knew that he had the finest army in the world—perhaps the finest the world had ever seen.

CHAPTER 6

Outbreak of the Seven Years' War

Failure of Frederick's Diplomacy

The European peace was shaky. By 1754 England and France, vying with each other for supremacy in colonial North America and India, were at the brink of war. This colonial rivalry was complicating the confused international rivalries on the continent of Europe.

Further complications were personal rivalries and feuds among the monarchs. Not the least of these was Maria Theresa's continuing hatred of Frederick and her determination to regain Silesia. Frederick had also created two other bitter feminine foes. His former admirer, the Czarina Elizabeth, had received reports of Frederick's witty but insulting remarks about her to his friends at Sans Souci and was determined to seek vengeance. He had been even more insulting in remarks about Madame de Pompadour, mistress of Louis XV of France, and she also wanted revenge.

Frederick had a reliable network of spies by which he kept informed of secret negotiations among other European powers, as these dealings affected Prussian interests. In 1755 he learned of a secret treaty, by which Austria and Russia agreed to defeat Prussia and then divide up the territory. Saxony and Sweden agreed to come into the conflict later and were to share in the spoils—getting their share of Prussia for their help. A buildup of troops in Russia, along the Prussian-Lithuanian border, was secretly reported to Frederick by his ardent admirer, young Grand Duke Peter, who was the nephew of Czarina Elizabeth, and married to Frederick's cousin Catherine.

Frederick realized that he would need a powerful ally, and had to choose between England and France. Partly because of the enmity of Madame de Pompadour, he finally selected England, and on January 16, 1756, signed the Neutrality Convention of Westminster. He felt that this was his only hope to counter the alliance of Austria and Russia. He realized that this alliance with France's most bitter foe, England, would alienate the French. But Frederick was sure that France would never ally herself with her other traditional European enemy, Austria.

However, when it came to choosing among traditional foes, France soon decided that England was the more dangerous. She quickly forgot her old quarrels with Austria and signed the Treaty of Versailles on May 1, 1756. By this treaty France and Austria each promised to send 24,000 men if the other was attacked.

As a result of alienating Russia, and miscalculating the French, combined with long-standing Prussian disputes with Austria and Sweden, Frederick was now faced by a coalition of every major European continental power: Austria, Sweden, Russia, and France. England's help would be useful, but she was completely absorbed in her colonial struggle overseas, and unwilling to send her own men to fight for Hanover, or anywhere else in Europe. Frederick's hopes of survival were grim.

During the summer of 1756 Frederick learned of Austrian and Russian plans to attack Prussia in the spring of 1757. Frederick tried to obtain an Austrian reassurance that there would be no such attack. But it soon became obvious that he would receive no reassurance. His enemies had decided to crush him and Prussia.

Frederick's Plan

Thereupon Frederick chose to take the initiative, rather than await the coalition attack. Austria, France, Sweden, Saxony, and Russia had together populations totaling about 100,000,-000 people, while Prussia, including Silesia, had about 4,500,-000. The combined allied resources were even more overwhelming. Frederick's only hope lay in winning a quick victory, and knocking some of the allies out of the coalition before they were ready for war. He knew that the allies had not yet reached agreement on some of the problems of coalition warfare, such as who should command, where each army should be sent, and the like.

The Prussian army was in readiness, whereas Frederick's opponents had not yet mobilized their forces. He stationed about 80,000 of his 150,000 men along the northern and eastern frontiers: in Pomerania to watch the Swedes, along the long Russian and Polish frontiers, and in Silesia, with a small garrison in Berlin.

With his remaining 70,000 men divided into three field armies, Frederick invaded Saxony on August 28, 1756. This was the beginning of the Seven Years' War.

Frederick commanded the central Prussian army, crossing the Elbe at Torgau. He gave command of the right to Duke Ferdinand of Hanover, who also had a small English-Hanoverian contingent. The left was commanded by Duke August Wilhelm of Brunswick-Bevern.

Frederick's plan was daring. The three Prussian forces were to unite to take Dresden and then march into Bohemia, where he expected to defeat the Austrian army. He then planned to invade Austria and seize Vienna. He hoped to reach Vienna before the enemy coalition could muster their combined forces and unify their command to deal with his invasion. To do this before winter required speed and precise coordination.

The Conquest of Saxony

The Saxon army of 14,000 evacuated Dresden, which was occupied by the Prussians on September 10. But the Saxons then retreated to an almost impregnable camp at Pirna, along the Elbe River and near the Bohemian border. Unable to assault the fortifications with adequate strength, Frederick had to resort to blockade.

Negotiations for surrender bogged down when Frederick demanded that Saxony and her army join him in an alliance against Austria. "Such terms are unheard of in all history," said the Saxon envoy.

"I try to be original," replied Frederick.

Meanwhile, an Austrian army was sent to aid the Saxons. Field Marshal Maximilian von Browne marched north from Prague on September 10 with about 45,000 men. When Frederick learned of this Austrian movement, he advanced up the Elbe from Pirna with his main body, leaving a force to maintain the blockade of the starving Saxons.

Battle of Lobositz

On October 1, the armies of Frederick and Marshal Browne met at Lobositz, on the Elbe, in the midst of the rugged Erzgebirge Mountains. The two generals brought about equal forces to combat—about 30,000 men each. The battle began in a thick fog, resulting in an uncoordinated series of local engagements in which the superiority of the Prussian infantry prevailed. After both sides had suffered about 3,000 casualties, the Austrians gave way and retreated into the mountains. Frederick decided not to pursue until he had dealt with the Saxons. He returned to the blockade of Pirna.

When the Saxons in Pirna heard the news of the Battle of Lobositz they surrendered. But by then it was October 14, too late for the whirlwind campaign Frederick had planned. With

93

winter approaching, and having lost the chance to sweep quickly through Bohemia, Frederick and the Prussian army settled down in Dresden to await spring.

During the winter Frederick took over the entire Saxon army and incorporated it into his own. He levied heavy taxes on the Saxon people, probably because he bitterly resented the fact that their determined opposition had ruined his plans, and had left him in a serious position indeed.

Invasion of Bohemia

By spring Frederick had increased his total force under arms to 175,000 men. About 60,000 of these continued to guard the frontiers with Swedish Pomerania and with Russia, and to provide garrisons for key points in Prussia and Silesia. Another 40,000 were in Hanover where they were combined with about 10,000 English-Hanoverian troops, under the command of Duke William Augustus of Cumberland, brother of King George II of England. Field Marshal von Schwerin had a force of about 10,000 in Silesia, and Duke August Wilhelm of Brunswick-Bevern had an equal force in southeastern Saxony. Frederick had concentrated his main army of about 50,000 men on the Elbe near Pirna.

Frederick was aware that his enemies were preparing to put a total of nearly 500,000 men into the field against him that year: more than 100,000 French, about 150,000 Russians, 150,000 Austrians, and the remainder made up of Swedish and smaller German contingents. But in April only the Austrians were ready, with more than 130,000 men in Bohemia. Frederick decided to deal first with the Austrians, and then to try to defeat his other enemies one at a time.

Late in April Frederick marched south up the Elbe into Bohemia. Schwerin and the Duke of Brunswick-Bevern were ordered to join him at Prague on May 6. Frederick's orders to them said that he expected a battle with the Austrians on that date.

Battle of Prague

Exactly on schedule the three contingents met just north of Prague early in the morning of May 6. Facing them, just east of the city, was Prince Charles's army of 70,000 men, entrenched in a strong position. Frederick, whose total force was now about 64,000, decided to attack at once.

Schwerin, who had arrived on time only because of a three-day forced march, protested that his men were dead tired. He asked for a delay, but Frederick rejected this idea because Austrian Field Marshal Count Leopold von Daun, with 60,000 additional Austrian troops, was known to be only 30 miles away from Prague. Frederick ordered Schwerin to move at once to form up in some meadows near the Austrian right flank. He was to hit the flank at right angles, while Frederick's main effort struck the right wing from the front.

Prince Charles's troops were drawn up on the crest of a

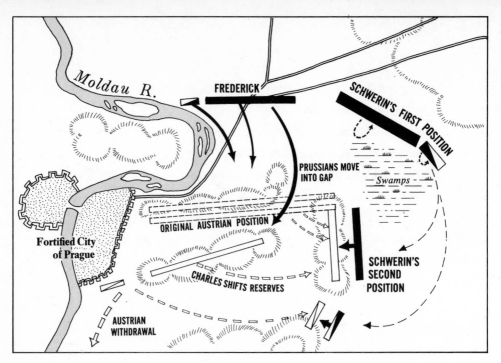

Battle of Prague

horseshoe ridge. The Austrian left flank was covered by the Elbe River and the defenses of Prague. The right flank was protected by a marsh. It was this marsh that Frederick had mistakenly identified as a meadow.

At about 10:00 A.M. the Prussian attack began. But as the Prussians clambered through the unexpectedly soggy ground, they were hit by volleys of Austrian artillery. Schwerin's troops were particularly hard hit. The Prussian attack was forced back. Schwerin led another charge and was killed by grapeshot. Frederick, seeing his old teacher of war fall at the head of his troops, was overcome with nausea.

96

Nevertheless, the Prussian pressure mounted against the Austrian right wing, and some of the Prussian cavalry, followed by infantry, worked their way around the swamps, to begin an envelopment of the Austrian right flank. Prince Charles ordered his reserves to move to the right, and shifted his right wing to meet this threat.

This move opened a gap in the right-center of the Austrian line. Frederick, seeing this, quickly seized his opportunity to throw in some infantry reserves, who soon widened the gap, and poured through. (Such a penetration of a unexpected gap in an enemy line has ever since been called "the Prague Maneuver.") Hit in flank and rear, the units of the Austrian right wing began to crumble, and confusion began to spread through the Austrian army. At this point Marshal Browne, the best Austrian leader on the field, was mortally wounded as he was trying to restore order. The Austrians fled.

About 40,000 Austrians reached the fortifications of Prague. Another 10,000 refugees finally reached Daun's army to the southeast. Total Austrian casualties were about 10,000 killed and wounded and 4,275 taken prisoners. Prussian losses were also high—11,740 killed and wounded and 1,560 prisoners. The victorious Prussians promptly laid siege to Prague.

It was probably the heavy losses suffered in the Battle of Prague which caused Frederick to begin to change his mind about one aspect of his tactical system. During the period between wars Frederick had decided that he should have his infantry advance rapidly to the attack without firing their muskets, for the same reasons that had caused him to eliminate firepower from his cavalry tactics. The infantrymen were to carry their muskets on their shoulders, and lower them only to use the bayonet when they reached the enemy line. He had written in his *Instructions*: "It is not fire but bearing which defeats the enemy. And because the decision is gained more quickly by always marching against the enemy than by amusing yourself firing, the sooner a battle is decided, the fewer men are lost in it."

The Battle of Prague, however, caused the king to revise his ideas about firepower. It was not long before he was saying: "Battles are won by superiority of fire." He was the first general to understand fully, and then to use, the modern concept of fire superiority.

Battle of Kolin

Strangely, for several weeks after the Battle of Prague, Daun did nothing, even though his army, combined with the garrison of Prague, outnumbered the Prussians by more than two to one. Finally, prodded by Maria Theresa, he began to advance toward Prague with about 60,000 men. Frederick, taking 34,000 men, all he could spare from the siege of Prague, marched southeastward to meet Daun. He left about 16,000 to hold the siege lines around the city.

Daun spent three days in choosing a base for his offensive against Prague. He finally selected the hills west of Kolin, along the highway to Prague from the east. On June 18, Frederick's army reached Daun's entrenched camp. The king decided to attack the Austrian right flank, as he had at the Battle of Prague. As usual, he employed the oblique march, in order to be able to outnumber the more numerous foe at the decisive point of attack. However, due to a combination of misunderstandings and unexpected Austrian vigor and initiative on the left flank, soon the whole Prussian army was involved in a general battle.

The Prussian infantry fought tenaciously against these odds, however. After Frederick had thrown in all of his reserves, his troops held a considerable portion of the heights where the Austrians had been entrenched. Daun now became discouraged and ordered a general retreat. However, the orders did not reach a large contingent of Saxon cavalry, in reserve on the Austrian right. Or, if the order was received, it was ignored. Now, five hours after the battle had begun, this fresh cavalry force struck the left flank of the exhausted Prussian infantry, who fell back. The Austrian infantry, encouraged by this unexpected development, renewed the struggle and pressed after the retreating Prussians.

In vain Frederick tried to rally his troops. Finally, when he was almost alone in front of the advancing Austrians, one of his staff officers persuaded him to leave the field with his retreating army.

Prussian losses were heavy—6,710 killed and wounded, 5,380 prisoners, and 45 guns. The total Austrian loss was 6,500 killed and wounded and 1,500 prisoners.

Skillfully Frederick reorganized his beaten troops, then marched back to Prague. Coolly and deliberately he withdrew from the siege lines around Prague, and in the first days of July marched back down the Elbe River into Saxony.

Frederick on the Run

The allied forces were growing, and they threatened Frederick's army and nation from every direction. There were now about 110,000 Austrians under Prince Charles and Marshal Daun in Bohemia; 100,000 Russians under Marshal Etienne Apraxin were invading East Prussia; 125,000 French were advancing into Hanover; 20,000 Swedes were in Pomerania; and 40,000 men in a newly collected Reich Army (composed of contingents of several small German states) were in central Germany, marching to join the French in Hanover. To oppose all of these armies Frederick had only about 60,000 men with him in Saxony; 30,000 more were in East Prussia, about 10,000 were in Brandenburg and Silesia, and the 54,000-man Prussian-Hanoverian army under the Duke of Cumberland was in Hanover.

As if the overwhelming odds against him were not enough, Frederick now found himself plagued by incompetence among his subordinates and his allies. His younger brother and heir, Prince Augustus William, was in command of a contingent of about 20,000 men retreating from northeastern Bohemia to Zittau, while Frederick, and the main body of 40,000, were retreating down the Elbe. Prince Charles, seeing an opportunity to cut off the smaller Prussian force, aggressively pursued and outmaneuvered Augustus William. After losing more than half his men, the prince finally joined Frederick at Dresden on July 29.

Frederick at once relieved his brother from command, saying that he deserved to be court-martialed and sentenced to death. He wrote to his brother, "You can commit as many follies as you please when I am gone, but this is the last while I am alive." Never again did Frederick see his brother, who died of shame and heartbreak within a year.

Meanwhile the inept Duke of Cumberland was defeated at the Battle of Hastenbeck on July 26 by the principal French army, under Marshal Louis d'Estrées. The Prussian contingent of Cumberland's army retreated into western Brandenburg. Cumberland himself abandoned Hanover and returned to England.

Then, on August 30, 1757, in East Prussia, General Lehwald was defeated by far superior Russian armies at the Battle of Gross-Jägersdorf, near Königsberg. With the remnants of his army Lehwald retreated from East Prussia, which was soon completely occupied by the Russians.

The allies now closed in on Prussia, confident that Frederick would soon be crushed by overwhelming numbers.

CHAPTER 7

Rossbach and Leuthen

March and Countermarch

Rather than becoming paralyzed under the impact of approaching disaster, Frederick skillfully redeployed his remaining forces to attempt to forestall invasions of Brandenburg from three directions: west, southwest, and south. His frequent letters to his sister Wilhelmina at this time often mentioned suicide, but he does not seem to have seriously contemplated it. He was spending twelve to fourteen hours each day in military planning and administration. Nonetheless, each night he found time to take his mind off his troubles by playing the flute and writing verses.

Frederick decided that the most immediate threats were the two French armies and the Reich Army, approaching Brandenburg from the west and southwest. Late in August Frederick marched west with about 25,000 men. He left the Duke of Brunswich-Bevern in command in Silesia, with about 15,000 men. Arriving in Leipzig on September 3, Frederick learned of the defeat of Lehwald at Gross-Jägersdorf. Thus there was now a threat to Brandenburg from a fourth direction: the east.

The most pressing danger was still the expected meeting of the three allied armies in western Brandenburg, however. The main French army of the Duke de Richelieu (who had replaced d'Estrées) was still in Hanover. But Duke Charles de Soubise's 24,000 French had already joined the 40,000-man Reich Army commanded by Prince Joseph of Saxe-Hildburghausen, and the combined forces had occupied Magdeburg. If these two armies met with that of Richelieu they could advance on Berlin with about 150,000 men.

Frederick continued west toward Magdeburg in a forced march, covering 170 miles in ten days. He hoped to provoke Hildburghausen and Soubise into a battle. But even though they had more than a two-to-one superiority, the allied generals refused to fight. They withdrew from Magdeburg and retreated southwestward to Eisenach. There does not seem to be any reason why they moved farther away from Richelieu's larger army in Hanover.

With his enemies in the west obviously hesitant and still divided, Frederick in early October dashed back to southeastern Saxony. Prince Charles and Daun had defeated Brunswick-Bevern at the Battle of Moys (near Gorlitz) and were threatening an invasion of Brandenburg from Bohemia through Saxony and Silesia. Brunswick-Bevern had been forced back into Silesia.

On October 16 an Austrian raiding party plundered the suburbs of Berlin. Frederick sent Prince Maurice of Anhalt-Dessau (son of the Old Dessauer) with a contingent of Prussians to Berlin. On October 18 they drove out the Austrian hussars.

By this time Frederick was marching west again with 21,000

men. The main Austrian army had halted its advance on Berlin when Frederick approached. But Soubise and Hildburghausen were again advancing. By the end of October Frederick was west of the Saale River, again endeavoring to entice Soubise and Hildburghausen into battle.

Battle of Rossbach

The Franco-Imperial army, now totaling nearly 60,000 men, commanded a good position on high ground west of the village of Rossbach. On November 5 Frederick formed up his army north of Rossbach. The allies, with nearly a three-to-one advantage, decided to accept his challenge. They planned to envelop the Prussian left flank, intending to swing completely around the Prussians with about 40,000 men in order to do so. The remaining 15,000 men were left in position opposite the Prussian line of battle.

Frederick watched this maneuver from a rooftop in Rossbach, and at first thought the allies were retreating. Finally he realized what they were doing and at once prepared for battle. He pretended to withdraw to the east from Rossbach, as though fearful of being cut off by the allied envelopment. Several hills hid the Prussian movement from the Franco-Imperial army, but it was supposed by the overconfident allies that Frederick was running away.

In fact, however, the Prussian cavalry, thirty-eight squadrons under General von Seydlitz, was swinging wide to the east and

Frederick watching the enemy manuevering at the Battle of Rossbach.
(New York Public Library, Picture Collection)

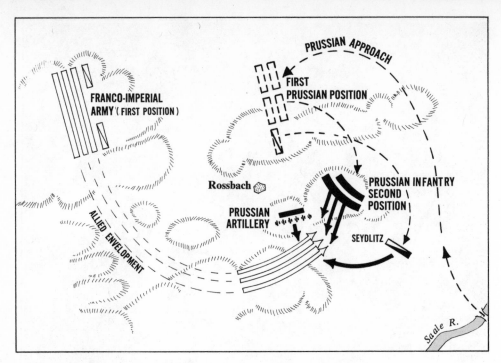

Battle of Rossbach

then south, while the infantry, much more mobile than the allied foot soldiers, shortly changed direction to the south, screened by the hills from allied observation. Meanwhile the allied army had completed its movement around the original Prussian flank and turned northeast to deploy.

Suddenly the head of the allied column was met in the left front by heavy Prussian artillery fire, supported by seven battalions of infantry. Soon after this the Prussian cavalry charged into the allied right flank, throwing the marching columns into confusion. The main body of the Prussian infantry then attacked the enemy mass, in oblique echelon from the left. One Prussian battalion after another smashed into the allied column. In less than an hour and a half the allied army was in confused flight, closely pursued by the Prussians until dark.

The allies suffered 8,400 casualties, while Frederick's losses were only 600. One of these was General Seydlitz, who had been badly wounded in leading the first charge.

At dawn next day, Frederick himself led his hussars and dragoons in continued pursuit of the retreating allies. He soon reached the French rear guard, which took up a delaying position in and around a chateau on the east bank of the Unstrut River. Frederick dismounted his dragoons; then, supported by horse artillery, led them as infantry in an attack on the chateau. He soon drove the French out and across the river.

Militarily this minor engagement is important in revealing Frederick's understanding of the proper employment of dragoons in their dual role. He knew when dragoons should use firearms, as well as when they should not. His actions also demonstrated the king's utter disregard for his own safety.

Word of the Battle of Rossbach quickly spread though Europe. It was also the first Prussian battle against the French, and it had been won against great odds. All Germany celebrated the victory, even those states on the imperial side. It was looked upon as a German victory over the French, who had made themselves more hated than ever by pillaging the countryside as they had moved toward Rossbach. Frederick became the most popular man in Germany. As Macaulay wrote, the reaction to the Battle of Rossbach showed that "the Germans were truly a nation."

As for Frederick, he was particularly pleased with the performance of his cavalry. Here was clear proof of the soundness of his doctrine, and the efficiency of his training.

Return to Silesia

Despite the prestige gained by his victory at Rossbach, Frederick's overall situation had been little improved. Brunswick-Bevern had been badly defeated at Breslau on October 22, and had been taken prisoner by Prince Charles. The Prussian army in Silesia, now under Ziethen, had been forced to withdraw east of the Oder, and then to retreat north toward Brandenburg. The Austrians now controlled most of Silesia.

Prussia's situation now seemed hopeless to Frederick's enemies, and to many of his own people as well. Prussia was open to attack from all directions, by armies vastly outnumbering his. But, as one historian has written, "Nothing was ever lost to Frederick till he had played his final card. He would rather die with his last grenadier at the foot of the Austrian lines then yield one inch of Silesia."

Frederick marched eastward from Rossbach toward Silesia, covering 180 miles in fifteen days. By the time he reached Parchwitz, near Liegnitz, on December 3, he had only 14,000 men with him. At Parchwitz he was met by Ziethen, with 18,000 troops. This total force of 32,000 men, more than half of whom were discouraged by defeat, and the remainder exhausted from marching, seemed insignificant against the 80,000 men with

Prince Charles at Breslau. The Austrians were amused by word of the approach of Frederick and his tiny army, which the Austrians called "the Potsdam Guard Company."

"We Must Beat the Enemy or Perish"

By evening of December 4 Frederick had decided to attack. That night he called his generals together and spoke to them simply and eloquently in words recorded by a junior staff officer.*

Gentlemen, you know our disasters. Schweidnitz and Breslau and a good part of Silesia are gone. . . . There would be nothing left but for my boundless trust in you and your courage. Each of you has distinguished himself by some memorable act. These services I know and remember.

The hour of decision is at hand. I shall have done nothing if I do not keep Silesia. I intend, in spite of all the rules of art, to seek Prince Charles, who has thrice our strength, and to attack him wherever I find him. It is not numbers I rely on, but your gallantry and whatever little skill I myself possess. This risk I must take or everything will be lost. We must beat the enemy, or perish every one of us before his guns.

Tell my determination to your officers, and prepare the men for the work to be done. I demand exact obedience

* There are differing translations of this speech. That quoted here is essentially the version in Theodore Ayrault Dodge's *Great Captains,* with some modifications based on Ludwig Reiner's *Frederick the Great.*

Frederick delivering his famous talk to his generals on the eve of the Battle of Leuthen. (New York Public Library, Picture Collection)

from you and from them. You are Prussians, and will act as such. But if any of you dreads to share my dangers, he may now have his discharge which I shall grant without a word of reproach.

There was a pause, as the king looked around the room where he and the generals were assembled. A smile must have come to his face as he heard a murmur from the officers, and saw them all pull theselves up proudly to attention.

"Ah, I knew it!" Frederick exclaimed. "Not one of you would desert me! With your help victory is sure. If I am left on the field, and not able to reward you for what you shall do tomorrow, our country will see to that. Now, go down to your lines and tell your regiments what I have said here. I demand again exact obedience, and I shall keep a close eye on each of them. The cavalry regiment which does not charge into the enemy the instant the order is given, I will unhorse and make a garrison regiment. The infantry battalion which, whatever it may encounter, pauses but an instant shall lose its colors and sabres, and I shall have the badges cut from its uniforms. And now, goodnight. By this time tomorrow we shall have beaten the enemy, or we shall never meet again."

The generals relayed Frederick's words of determination to their officers and men. The small Prussian army settled itself for the cold night in the grim resolve to destory the Austrian army, or be destroyed trying. Frederick, as had been his custom during the marches across Germany, spent the night beside several campfires, finally sleeping with a group of his proud grenadiers, until he was awakened by an aide at 3:00 A.M.

111

Approach to Combat

By 4:00 A.M. on December 5, 1757, the Prussian army was trudging through the darkness on the road to Breslau, its front and flanks covered by a cavalry screen. It was still dark when the Prussian advance guard cavalry overran an Austrian outpost at Neumarkt, to discover an Austrian field bakery guarded by 1,000 Croats. The cavalry attacked, capturing 500 Croats and 10,000 loaves of freshly baked bread.

When Frederick received word of this unexpected capture, he realized for the first time that Charles had left his entrenched camp at Breslau, and was coming out to meet the Prussians. The Austrian general had sent his bakery on ahead, planning to halt and feed Sunday breakfast to his troops at Neumarkt. Laughingly Frederick ordered his army to halt for an hour to enjoy the holiday meal that had been intended for the enemy. Then, about dawn, shortly after 7:00 A.M., the Prussian army resumed its march toward Breslau.

Meanwhile fugitives from Neumarkt had warned Charles of the Prussian approach. The prince, who had rejected the advice of Marshal Daun when he had elected to move out to meet Frederick on the open battlefield, now found his confidence slightly shaken. But he knew that Frederick could not have many more than 30,000 men, while he had 80,000, who had won their last two battles against the Prussians. He halted just west of Lissa and the Schweidnitz River, to form a battle line between the villages of Nypern and Sageschutz, just east of Leuthen.

Frederick, as usual during an approach to combat, was riding with the advance guard cavalry. At the village of Borna, 5 miles from Leuthen, and about 10 from Breslau, they suddenly saw a cavalry outpost in the mist ahead. Putting spurs to his horse, Frederick personally led an enveloping attack, which captured most of the 500 Saxon dragoons. A few survivors got back to Leuthen, but their confused story convinced Charles that this was merely a Prussian reconnaissance party.

While Charles was thinking about this, Frederick had ridden ahead to Scheuberg Hill, northernmost of a line of hills just east of Borna. From there he could see the Austrian army, deployed in a double line over a distance of 5 miles on the rolling ground to his front. He sent the advance guard cavalry to occupy the entire line of hills, which was parallel to the Austrian line. At the same time, with his spyglass, he quickly assessed the Austrian dispositions. In a few minutes, he had prepared his plan of battle, and sent back orders to the column of troops still marching down the road toward him.

The Austrian right flank was protected by swampy ground. But the center and left of the Austrian line was on open, firm ground which the king knew well. He saw that the enemy's extreme left wing was bent back at an angle, to be ready for a possible Prussian envelopment. The Austrians had learned by experience to expect such a maneuver from Frederick.

113

Frederick sent his advance guard cavalry forward, under General George Wilhelm von Driessen, to demonstrate against the Austrian right and center. The remainder of the army was marched to the right, in a double column, behind the line of hills. Frederick issued orders that upon his command the entire infantry column should march to the left, and then attack near the angle of the Austrian left wing in the oblique order which they had so often practiced. Leading the column was Ziethen's cavalry.

Charles had originally placed his reserve behind the left flank, where he considered a typical Frederick flank attack was most likely. But his right-wing commander, General Lucchesi, observing the Prussian advance guard cavalry demonstrating in front of him, was certain that the attack would hit his flank. He appealed to have the reserves moved behind him. Daun, the second-in-command, refused this appeal at first, but by 10:00 A.M., as more Prussian cavalry appeared in front of the right wing, both he and Charles decided that Frederick was planning to attack that wing. The reserves were shifted, the movement being completed by noon.

It was only a few minutes later that Frederick issued the command for his entire army to march to its left flank. The double column now became a double line, which quickly became an oblique double line, as each battalion marched parallel to the one to its right, but fifty paces behind. The movement was made with clockwork precision, as though the troops were on the Potsdam parade ground.

Now the Prussian artillery galloped through the gaps between battalions to take up position opposite the angle in the Austrian line. As the infantry swept past, the massed guns were already hammering at the hasty entrenchments which the Austrians had prepared. And at this moment, about 1:00 P.M., Ziethen and his cavalry charged the Austrian left.

Trying to forestall the feared effects of a Prussian cavalry charge, the Austrian left-flank cavalry countercharged downhill against the attackers. But the Prussians had a slight numerical superiority. Although they hesitated briefly under the Austrian blow, Ziethen's men were supported by their horse artillery, and by the infantry sweeping up on their left and right. The Prussian troopers soon drove the Austrian cavalry back into their lines.

By this time the combination of artillery pummeling and the successive shocks of the echeloned Prussian infantry battalions had broken through the angle of the Austrian left wing. Now, with battalion shock succeeding battalion shock, the Prussian battalions wheeled to their left. They began to roll up the entire Austrian left wing. At the same time Ziethen's horsemen were ripping into the small remaining portion of the Austrian wing east of the angle. By 2:00 P.M. Ziethen was capturing entire regiments; the Austrian left was hopelessly smashed.

There is a legend that at this point in the battle Prince Maurice became worried about the losses suffered by the ex-

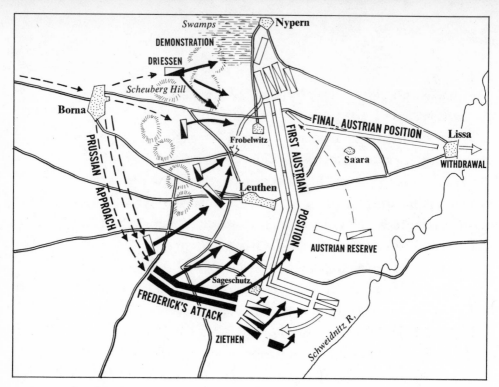

Battle of Leuthen

treme right wing units of Prussian infantry, who had opened the battle. He ordered them to fall back to the reserves to get a brief rest. "Damn the reserves," the soldiers shouted. "Send more ammunition. We need it badly." The advance continued.

Charles and Daun valiantly tried to reestablish a new line north and east of Leuthen. After all, they still had fresh troops outnumbering the Prussians by two to one. Although the sudden readjustment of the position had caused considerable confusion in the Austrian lines, the Prussians, now attacking due north, were clearly slowing down.

At this point Frederick threw in his last reserves. The Prussian artillery, keeping up with the advancing infantry, blasted great gaps in the massed Austrian lines. The Prussian advance again began to gain momentum.

Now General Lucchesi led the Austrian right-flank cavalry, bolstered by the reserve cavalry, in a charge against the left flank of the Prussian infantry advancing past Leuthen. But Frederick had anticipated this possibility. He had held out General von Driessen's cavalry—the original advance guard—with orders to wait behind Scheuberg Hill until the Austrian right-flank cavalry was committed. When the Austrian squadrons rode past their hiding place, Driessen and his men charged out to hit the enemy horsemen in the flank and rear. The Austrian cavalry scattered, Lucchesi was killed, and the Prussian advance continued.

Charles ordered another withdrawal, and attempted to stand again near the village of Saara. But by this time his men were in no mood to await the steady Prussian advance. A few Prussian artillery volleys scattered the remaining Austrians. The fugitives fled east, pursued by Prussian cavalry.

The battle had ended by 4:00 P.M. Frederick had defeated his enemy in three hours of fighting. Nightfall alone permitted most of the vanquished to escape across the Schweidnitz River toward Breslau.

Frederick himself, leading two grenadier battalions, and accompanied by aides carrying lanterns, followed the enemy as far as the village of Lissa. There he found many Austrians, who surrendered to him. He joined a group of astonished enemy

A Prussian assault during the Battle of Leuthen. (*New York Public Library, Picture Collection*)

officers, in a private home, as they were having supper. While his two battalions camped in the fields near Lissa, the king spent the night on a pile of straw, in a house surrounded by a few guards and hundreds of enemy prisoners.

Next morning Frederick learned that his army had lost 6,200 men killed and wounded in the brief but bloody struggle. Austrian losses were about 7,000 killed and wounded, and 12,000 prisoners, of whom perhaps 3,000 were wounded. The Prussians captured 116 guns and 51 regimental colors. Within the next two weeks another 20,000 prisoners were rounded up from the countryside, and in Breslau. When Prince Charles and the remnants of his army reached Königgrätz, in Bohemia, a few days later, he had only 37,000 men, and of these only 15,000 were fit for duty.

Frederick the Great is generally acknowledged to have been the greatest tactician of modern history. Leuthen was undoubtedly his finest battle. No operation has ever been more brilliantly planned, or more perfectly executed. Every development, expected and unexpected, was flexibly and promptly handled by the king and by his men just as though they were on maneuvers or on parade. Napoleon later described the battle as a "masterpiece of maneuver and resolution."

CHAPTER 8

Zorndorf to Kunersdorf

A Respite

The Battles of Rossbach and Leuthen had accomplished the impossible. The enemies who had been about to overwhelm tiny Prussia had not only been halted, they had been thrown back. The French and Austrian commanders were demoralized, and were reluctant to initiate further campaigns against Frederick. In fact, his enemies never forgot the miracle accomplished by Frederick between November 5 and December 5, 1757.

The French were also occupied by their overseas war. William Pitt, who had been out of power, had returned as British Prime Minister, to direct an ever more aggressive prosecution of the colonial struggles. He was determined to drive the French out of North America and India. He also granted Frederick a yearly subsidy, which was sufficient to equip and maintain 50,000 additional men in the Prussian army. In return, Frederick sent one of his best generals, his brother-in-law Prince Ferdinand of Brunswick, to lead an English-German army against the French in Hanover.

Frederick hoped that his victories might bring a permanent

peace. And for a while it appeared that he might get it. Maria Theresa was willing to give up Silesia. France was desperate for peace on the Continent, in order to fight Britain overseas. But vengeful Elizabeth of Russia reunited her allies against Frederick.

Russian Invasion of East Prussia

Russia was the only allied power ready to operate seriously against Frederick early in 1758. Elizabeth had removed General Apraxin, who had failed to take advantage of his victory at Gross-Jägersdorf, and replaced him with General Count Wilhelm Fermor.

In January a force of 31,000 Russians again entered East Prussia, but they were soon bogged down by muddy roads. The Swedish forces were similarly contained by the melting snows and muddy roads in Pomerania. Frederick decided, therefore, to move against the Austrians in Bohemia, to prevent them from recovering too soon from the defeats of the previous year. Then, when he turned to deal with the Russians in midsummer, the Austrians would not be able to threaten his rear.

The main Austrian army, commanded by Daun, lay about Königgratz. In April, Frederick sent his younger brother Prince Henry, with about 30,000 men, to keep Daun pinned down in northern Bohemia. Frederick himself took 40,000 men to invade Moravia.

Frederick proceeded to Olmütz, which he besieged until the

end of June. The prosecution of the siege was hampered by harassment of his line of communications by partisans under young Austrian General Gideon von Laudon. This culminated in late June in the capture of one of Frederick's supply convoys. By this time, furthermore, the Russians had consolidated their hold on East Prussia, and Fermor was preparing to invade Brandenburg. Reluctantly Frederick gave up the siege of Olmütz and prepared to march north before Fermor could cross the Oder.

Frederick's subsequent movements were so rapid and well concealed that the allies did not know where he would turn up next. Partly to confuse his foes, and partly as a typical joke, he marched northwest through central Bohemia. Daun, surprised by this bold move, came out of his fortified camp at Königgratz in a confused and clumsy effort to block the Prussian advance. Frederick then marched rapidly around Daun's army and seized the empty Austrian camp. After his men had eaten their fill of Austrian food and he had stocked his baggage wagons with Austrian supplies, Frederick resumed his march northward into Silesia. He left approximately half of his army in northern Silesia, under the command of Marshal Keith. With 14,000 men he went on by very rapid marches to reach the Oder River south of Frankfort-on-Oder by August 20. There he learned that the small Prussian force defending eastern Brandenburg was being besieged at Küstrin by Fermor and 52,000 Russians.

Frederick gathered all available forces between Berlin and the Oder, giving him a strength of about 33,000 men. He con-

centrated this army on the west bank of the Oder opposite
Küstrin and prepared to cross. Then when Fermor moved to oppose the crossing, Frederick made a rapid night march to the
north, where he had secretly collected boats several miles below Küstrin. He crossed there in a few hours early on Ausust 23,
and put himself on Fermor's line of communication. Fermor,
raising the siege, turned and moved to a defensive position on
high ground near the hamlet of Zorndorf. Because of the nature of the ground, the Russians were arrayed in an oblong
formation, facing north.

Battle of Zorndorf

On August 24, 1758, Frederick moved eastward, then south,
completely around the Russian position. Fermor hastily shifted
his front to the south, early on August 25, just as the Prussians
struck the southwest and southern sides of his formation in a
typical oblique order attack. Frederick did not have a very high
opinion of the Russians, so he was surprised by the savage Russian defense. Fermor's troops repulsed the initial Prussian attack. Seydlitz and his cavalry charged across marshy ground beyond the left flank of the Prussian infantry, to strike a paralyzing
blow against the Russian right. This gave Frederick an opportunity to re-form his shaken infantry. He shifted his front to the
east, and shortly after noon attacked the southeast corner of
the Russian position.

This attack was also repulsed. But Seydlitz had re-formed his

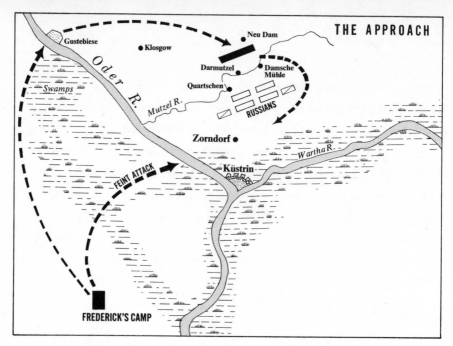

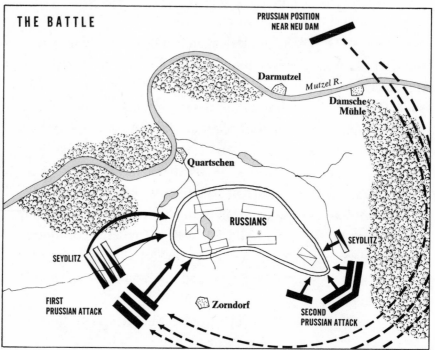

Battle of Zorndorf

cavalry, and again charged into the Russian infantry, this time on the Prussian right flank. Frederick's infantry assaulted once more, and an inconclusive butchery followed, ending only when nightfall put a stop to the fighting. By this time the Russian army had been nearly destroyed, having lost about 25,000 men killed and wounded, at least 50 percent of their fighting strength. But Frederick had lost 12,000, 40 percent of his army.

Early next morning Fermor and his surviving troops retreated to the northeast, abandoning 130 guns. But Frederick's troops were too exhausted and too disorganized to pursue. But by evening of August 26, Frederick had reorganized his army and was prepared to attack again next day.

At dawn, however, the Russians continued their retreat toward Königsberg (Kaliningrad). Frederick decided to let them go. He had learned a lot about the Russians, and was satisfied to see their threat ended, without having to fight another battle like Zorndorf.

The Battle of Zorndorf was perhaps the most bitterly contested struggle of the eighteenth century. Rarely have armies suffered such enormous casualties and still remained intact. Frederick singled Seydlitz out for special praise. He stated publicly that the Prussian victory had been due entirely to his two timely and successful cavalry charges.

Frederick had meanwhile received word that, in his absence, Daun had marched north from Bohemia into Saxony. The Austrian army was threatening the tiny force Frederick had left under his brother Prince Henry of Prussia, not far from Dresden. With about 15,000 men, Frederick marched back across the Oder toward Saxony by forced marches, making 22 miles a day. On learning of his approach, the Austrians withdrew on September 12.

Daun next took up positions near Hochkirch, his army of 90,000 blocking the road to Silesia from Saxony. Other Austrian troops besieged the Prussian garrison of Neisse. After joining his brother, Frederick had an army of 37,000 men. He briefly rested his troops, then marched east to regain control of Silesia. When he arrived in front of the Austrian entrenched camp at Hochkirch, Frederick boldly advanced to within a mile of Daun's lines, then put his own army into camp in a valley below the Austrians.

Field Marshal Keith, alarmed by the exposed position Frederick had selected, commented: "The Austrians deserve to be hanged if they don't attack us here." With typical quick wit the king replied: "They fear us worse than the gallows."

But bold General von Laudon was willing to challenge the Prussian hangman. After the armies had faced each other for four days, he finally persuaded the cautious Daun that the Prussian position was indefensible.

During the night of October 13–14 the Austrians silently

surrounded the Prussian camp. At dawn they attacked through a thick fog. The Prussians had not expected the attack, but as usual, Frederick's outposts were alert. The initial Austrian assault was repulsed, and a desperate struggle ensued. Despite the vigor of the Prussian counterattacks, the more numerous Austrians closed in steadily. The battle had raged for four hours when a charge by Ziethen's cavalry swept away one portion of the converging Austrian army. Realizing that his situation was desperate, Frederick decided to withdraw through the gap opened by Ziethen's horsemen. The withdrawal was made in good order.

Prussian losses were heavy—9,450 killed, wounded, or captured. Among the dead was Marshal Keith; among the prisoners were Prince Maurice, badly wounded, and Duke Francis of Brunswick. Left behind in the retreat were 101 Prussian guns. But the desperate Prussian defense had taken its toll. The Austrians suffered 8,000 casualties. Obstinately Frederick camped 4 miles from the battlefield and dared Daun to renew the struggle. The Austrian field marshal declined.

It was probably his recollection of Hochkirch that later prompted Frederick to remark that it is no disgrace to be defeated, but that it is unpardonable to be surprised.

Within three days of the disaster, Frederick had received reinforcements from Dresden. He commented to an aide: "The Marshal [Daun] has let us out of check; the game is not yet lost." He was again ready to take the offensive—but this time with more caution.

In a surprise march, the king slipped around Daun's right

and marched into Silesia. Facing northward he again dared Daun to attack. At the same time he sent a detachment to the aid of the beleaguered garrison of Neisse. Daun hesitated, then withdrew into Saxony. On October 23 the Austrian besiegers of Neisse hastily retreated to Bohemia. In a few days all of Silesia was again in Prussian hands.

Meanwhile Daun had laid siege to Dresden. Now that Silesia was again under control, Frederick followed the Austrians into Saxony. On November 15 Daun raised the siege of Dresden and retreated back to Bohemia.

Strategy and Fun

By winter Frederick had regained control of all of his possessions except East Prussia, and had again occupied Saxony. At the same time Ferdinand and his Anglo-Prussian army were firmly established in Hanover. By a combination of skill and unceasing activity, Frederick had actually strengthened his strategic position in northern Germany. He had also gained a formidable reputation which made the allies ever more reluctant to force him into battle. But his losses had been severe. In three years of fighting and marching he had lost 100,000 of his well-trained and disciplined troops. He could still put 150,000 men in the field, but at least half of his troops were recruits. During the winter, however, intensive training improved his new soldiers, although they were far from being the invincible Prussians of 1756.

During the winter of 1758–59, Frederick displayed a financial wizardry comparable to his military skill. He arranged his scanty finances to equip, supply, and maintain his armies. Yet he also had time not only for his usual flute concerts and unending verse composition, but also for poking a bit of fun at his enemies. He had learned that Austrian Field Marshal Daun had received a gift of a consecrated, or specially blessed, hat and sword from the Pope. (Some historians believe that there was no truth to the story, and that it had been planted originally by Frederick in a Dutch newspaper.) Whatever the source, the story provided Frederick another chance to display his biting wit.

First, in both French and Latin, he wrote out the kind of letter which he thought the Pope might send to Daun with such gifts: "May this sword . . . serve to destroy for ever those heresies. . . . May it drink the blood of rebels. . . ." And more in the same bloodthirsty, mock-religious tone.

When the letter was circulated around Europe, many people thought that the Pope had really written it. So pleased was Frederick with the results that he wrote another mock letter, which was supposed to be congratulations to Daun from French General Soubise. The principal passage was as follows:

"It is a pity that the Holy Father did not confer these gifts on you earlier. At Rossbach I was badly in need of a consecrated hat and sword, and I don't think they would have done you any harm at Leuthen."

129

By the spring of 1759 there was a cordon of 350,000 allied troops surrounding beleaguered Prussia, Hanover, and Saxony. Frederick with about 50,000 men was in Silesia, observing Daun's army in northern Bohemia. The remainder of his forces were scattered to oppose the other principal threats—from Russia, from Swedish Pomerania, and from France.

Duke Ferdinand of Brunswick, reinforced by British troops, had during the winter firmly established himself on the line Münster-Paderborn-Cassel. In the spring, at Frederick's direction, he advanced southwestward against the French, who were based on Frankfort and Wesel. But the French, under Marquis Louis de Contades, were too strong for him, and forced Ferdinand to retire across the Weser. The pursuing French seized the bridges at Minden, where they occupied a position too strong for direct attack.

On August 1, 1759, Ferdinand enticed the French to battle outside Minden. Contades commanded 60,000 troops as opposed to Ferdinand's 45,000. The Prussians and the small British contingent repulsed French attacks, then advanced victoriously. Only the incompetence and disobedience of British Lord Sackville, who commanded the British cavalry, enabled the French to retreat unhindered from the field.* Ferdinand pursued them almost to the Rhine. Then he had to stop, in

---

* Despite this disgraceful conduct, Sackville later became Lord Germain and displayed equal ineptness in controlling British military operations from London during the American Revolution.

order to be able to send reinforcements to help Frederick, who had encountered disaster in the east.

Disaster at Kunersdorf

General Peter S. Soltikov had replaced Fermor in command of the Russian army in East Prussia. In the early summer of 1759 he took the field with 70,000 men against the contingent of 26,000 Prussians that was covering the eastern approaches to Brandenburg and the Oder. Prussian General Karl Heinrich von Weddell, who commanded this defending army, thought that Frederick wanted him to attack the Russians. On July 23 he foolishly attacked Soltikov at Kay, on the banks of the Oder, and was badly defeated.

Now Frederick discovered that Daun had sent a force of 20,000 men, under Laudon, to join Soltikov for a joint invasion of Brandenburg. Leaving half of his army in Saxony, under his brother Henry, Frederick rushed to intercept Laudon, but was too late. The king then continued on to Frankfort, where he joined Weddell and other detachments in early August. By this time he had assembled 48,000 men with which to meet the allied army of 80,000 approaching from the east.

On August 12 Frederick crossed the Oder at Frankfort to seek battle with the Austrian-Russian army. The allies, learning of Frederick's approach, had taken up an entrenched position in the sandhills near Kunersdorf, 4 miles east of the river.

Despite his enemy's great numerical superiority, Frederick

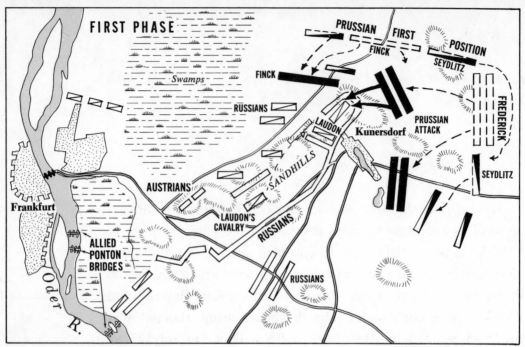

FIRST PHASE

Swamps

PRUSSIAN FIRST POSITION

FINCK

SEYDLITZ

FINCK

RUSSIANS

LAUDON

Kunersdorf

SANDHILLS

PRUSSIAN ATTACK

FREDERICK

AUSTRIANS

LAUDON'S CAVALRY

RUSSIANS

SEYDLITZ

Frankfurt

ALLIED PONTON BRIDGES

RUSSIANS

Oder R.

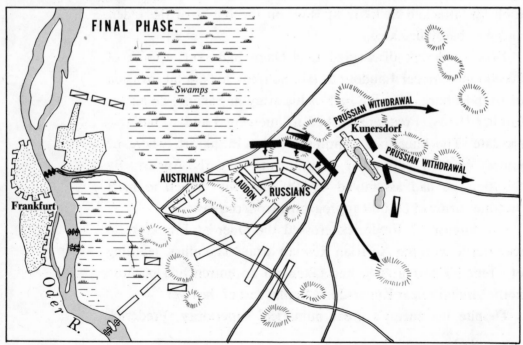

FINAL PHASE

Swamps

PRUSSIAN WITHDRAWAL

Kunersdorf

PRUSSIAN WITHDRAWAL

AUSTRIANS

LAUDON

RUSSIANS

Frankfurt

Oder R.

Battle of Kunersdorf

attempted a double envelopment. But Frederick's troops were not up to the complicated maneuver, and he had lost many of his best officers in the three preceding years. His columns lost their way in the woods and their attacks were delivered piecemeal. Nevertheless, after a few hours of fighting, some success had been gained, and the Prussians held parts of the enemy position. His generals—even impetuous Seydlitz—now urged Frederick to halt the attacks. The enemy would certainly retreat during the night.

But Frederick would be satisfied with nothing less than full victory. Remembering what he had written about Prussian troops in his *Instructions*, he insisted on continuing the attacks. Although the Prussians displayed courage and resourcefulness, they had been exhausted by hours of marching and fighting. They were repulsed in their efforts to take the remaining allied entrenchments. Then Laudon's fresh cavalry bore down on them, and the Prussian infantry formations crumbled. In a few minutes much of the Prussian army was in flight.

During this rout, Frederick had two horses shot out from under him, and a bullet crushed a snuffbox in his pocket. Close to despair, he exclaimed: "Will none of these blasted bullets hit me?" At one point, he was almost captured by Russian cavalry. But some of Ziethen's troopers formed a circle around him, and hacked their way out of the trap, while one officer led Frederick's horse.

The Prussians lost 20,752 men, 178 guns, and 28 colors in this disaster. It was the worst defeat Frederick had ever suffered and the first time his Prussian army had left a field in disorder.

133

That night Frederick wrote to his old tutor, General von Finckenstein, commanding in Berlin: "My coat is riddled with bullets. My misfortune is that I am still alive. Our losses are very considerable; of an army of 48,000 men I have, as I write, not 3,000 left."

It was not that bad, but it was bad enough.

The allies, however, did not follow up their victory. They had suffered over 16,000 casualties, but they should not have allowed this to deter them. They had won the war, and they should have realized it. All that was needed was a vigorous push to Berlin.

Frederick certainly believed that the war was lost. He gave command of the army to Lieutenant General Friedrich August von Finck; apparently he was ready to abdicate in favor of Prince Henry. But when the Prussian fugitives straggled back after the battle, and 12,000 reinforcements arrived from Ferdinand, Frederick again took heart. He decided to continue the struggle, and resumed command of his army.

Suddenly the king was the Frederick of old. In a series of sparkling maneuvers in northeastern Saxony, he and his brother foiled Daun's clumsy efforts to join his army with the Russians. Finally, having exhausted all his food and forage, Soltikov withdrew to Poland. Frederick could concentrate again on Daun's army.

Daun, who had been reinforced by the Reich Army, had retreated to a camp near Dresden. Frederick marched rapidly into central Saxony. He was determined to get the Austrians out of the country. He ordered General Finck to take a detachment of 12,000 men to get behind the Austrian army. Finck, and all of Frederick's other generals in the field, cautioned the king that his still-shaken army was not yet ready to take the offensive. But Frederick brushed aside these doubts. He repeated his order for Finck to move to Maxen, south of Dresden.

Daun promptly concentrated 42,000 men against Finck's isolated force. On November 21, 1759, the Austrians attacked and surrounded Finck's command. After two days of hard and costly fighting, Finck surrendered with all the survivors. By his obstinacy Frederick lost 12,000 men killed, wounded, or captured with all their equipment.

When General Finck was later released by the Austrians, Frederick had him tried by a court-martial and imprisoned for a year. He was dismissed in disgrace from the army and forced to take the blame for the Battle of Maxen. Frederick's treatment of Finck was shameful. Finck had done his best. Had Frederick himself commanded the detachment, the disaster might have been avoided. But he should have known better than anyone that there was only one Frederick.

CHAPTER 9

Desperation, Disaster, and Victory

Allied Offensive

During the severe winter of 1759–60 the allied coalition began to unify. Encouraged by the victories of Kunersdorf and Maxen, they had developed an offensive campaign plan for the spring and summer of 1760. Meanwhile Austrian and Hungarian light and irregular troops increased the tempo of their raids into Silesia.

One of these raids added to Frederick's growing feeling of gloom and discouragement. The Austrians captured General Ernst Heinrich von Czetteritz in a minor engagement on February 21. With him they found a copy of Frederick's *Instructions*, which the general had brought into the field, despite the king's orders. Frederick feared that the captured document would reveal all of his strategic plans for the defense of Prussia, as well as give his enemies a valuable insight into his methods of warfare.

In fact, the allies probably were inspired to some extent by the captured *Instructions* in developing their plan of campaign. The principal effort was to be against Brandenburg. Three columns were to converge against Frederick: Daun in Saxony with 100,000 men; Laudon in Silesia with 50,000; and Soltikov with 50,000 Russians in East Prussia. Other allied forces, totaling perhaps 50,000 more men, were to maintain constant pressure around the southern, eastern, and northern borders of Prussia and Silesia. At the same time, 125,000 French troops were to invade Hanover, then push on into Brandenburg from the west.

The allies, however, were still respectful of the prowess of Frederick. They agreed that whenever the king turned against one of their armies, the threatened one would retreat, while the others pressed on toward Berlin. In that way they hoped to wear Frederick and his Prussians down, and then concentrate overwhelming force against them near Berlin.

To counter the planned invasion Frederick faced Daun on the Elbe River with 40,000 men. Prince Henry had 34,000 in Silesia, and 15,000 additional Prussian soldiers opposed Russian-Swedish forces ravaging Pomerania. In Hanover, Duke Ferdinand had a Prussian-British army of 70,000 facing the French.

The allies began their converging advance in June, but their strategy did not work as planned. The Russians were soon halted by the maneuvering of Prince Henry, while Frederick kept Daun occupied in Saxony. However, this left Silesia open, and Austrian General Laudon defeated a Prussian detachment of 13,000 men under General Ernst Fouqué at Landshut on June 23. Laudon immediately invested Breslau.

Frederick began shuttling back and forth between Laudon

and Daun. When Daun moved to help Laudon, Frederick marched past him and on July 12 besieged Dresden. Daun came hurrying back to relieve Dresden, and almost surrounded Frederick. But the king slipped away in the nick of time on July 29. That same day, Glatz fell to Laudon's troops. The allied ring was tightening. Frederick, summoning Prince Henry's army to join him, plunged into Silesia to restore the situation in that province.

Battle of Liegnitz

Before Henry could reach him, however, Frederick, with about 25,000 men, was surrounded on three sides by Laudon and Daun, who had 90,000. Furthermore, 30,000 Russians, under General Czernichev, were hastening to join the Austrians, and were only three days away on the evening of August 14.

Frederick had received an intelligence report that the Austrians were planning a night attack. Secretly he withdrew from his camp after dark, leaving the fires burning so the Austrians would think the Prussians were still there. He arranged his men in battle order on the crescent of hills behind Liegnitz by 3:00 A.M. Then, sitting on top of a drum, he dozed.

Meanwhile Laudon with 35,000 men was also moving quietly in the darkness toward the same hill position that Frederick had occupied. He was planning to attack the Prussian camp at dawn. Frederick's outposts were alert, and when

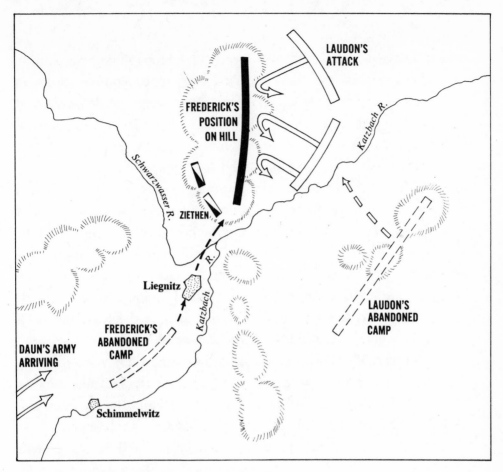

Battle of Liegnitz

Laudon's men started up the hill, they were greeted by Prussian artillery. The Austrians, however, were confident of their numerical superiority and continued the attack. For two and a half hours the battle raged in the darkness. By dawn Laudon's men had been driven away, having suffered 10,000 men killed and wounded, compared with 2,000 Prussian casualties.

Daun, several miles southwest, had been planning a frontal attack against the Prussians at dawn, to be coordinated with Laudon's attack from the rear. But when he learned that Laudon had been disastrously defeated, Daun ordered an immediate retreat. The Prussians marched on to Breslau, entering the city with bands playing, and colors flying proudly.

Meanwhile Frederick had given a false message to a peasant, telling him to get himself captured by the Russians. The peasant obeyed the order, and soon Czernichev was reading the letter. It was a message in Frederick's handwriting, supposedly intended for Prince Henry. Frederick wrote that the Austrians were fleeing in complete disorder, that Laudon had been killed, and that Frederick planned to move against the Russians. This was enough for Czernichev. He withdrew into Poland.

Frederick's victory at Liegnitz had done little more than assure his survival for a few more weeks. He realized that he probably could not survive another defeat, and that he had little to gain from even a brilliant victory against one portion of his enemies. But he also knew that inactivity would be worse than defeat. He resumed maneuvering against Daun, who was now advancing into Saxony.

On October 9 Austrian and Russian raiders seized and partly burned Berlin. Frederick marched toward his capital. The news of his approach alone caused the Russians to withdraw to Poland, and the Austrians into Saxony, after an occupation of three days.

Frederick turned south again, having decided that the time had come to deal boldly with Daun. The Austrian army, 66,000 strong, was in an almost inaccessible position—facing in all directions on the hills west of Torgau, along the Elbe River. Four hundred cannon were emplaced along the powerful earthworks that crowned the heights.

At the end of October, Frederick crossed the Elbe, planning an envelopment and simultaneous attacks from the front and rear against the Austrian fortified camp. He had been able to scrape together 44,000 troops. On November 2 he called his generals together. His purpose, as he told them, was "not to ask your advice, but to inform you that tomorrow I shall attack Marshal Daun."

Frederick explained his plan. He would lead about half of his army some 14 miles in a wide sweep to the west of Torgau to attack the northern, and rear, side of the Austrian fortifications. He entrusted the frontal attack by the remainder of the army to General Ziethen, whose force had about 7 miles to march. Ziethen was to start the battle by attracting the enemy's attention about noon. Frederick would make the main attack when he heard the sound of Ziethen's guns.

Frederick marched off at 6:30 on the bleak and snowy morning of November 3, 1760, his force divided into three columns: one was commanded by Frederick himself, the others by Generals von Hulsen and von Holstein. They were to travel on parallel routes through dense woods. Frederick had hoped to attack about noon, but all of the columns were delayed by the heavy snowfall.

Despite the difficulties of the march, Frederick's column of 8,000 men reached the assigned attack position at 1:00 P.M. There was no sign of the other columns. Nor was there any sound of firing to show that Ziethen was attacking. Frederick waited for the other two columns until 2:00 P.M., when he heard cannon fire to the south. He assumed that this was Ziethen's attack and so he decided to attack the rear of the Austrian position alone, with his own single column. He felt sure that the other two columns would march to the sound of the guns.

As a matter of fact, Ziethen was not attacking the main Austrian army. He was a superb and dashing cavalry commander, but he had never before been entrusted with a major combined arms force in an independent mission. He had been diverted from his objective by Austrian light troops while moving into attack position. He had fired on this small party and then, like a true, single-minded cavalryman, he gave chase, forgetting about Frederick's battle plan. It was the sound of this skirmish which led Frederick to attack.

Thus Frederick was advancing with 8,000 men against an entrenched garrison of more than 60,000. Nearly half of the Austrian artillery concentrated against the tiny assault column, and only about 2,000 of Frederick's grenadiers reached Daun's infantry line. There they inflicted serious losses, but they were driven back by overwhelming numbers. Prussian artillery batteries hurrying to support the infantry were destroyed by the

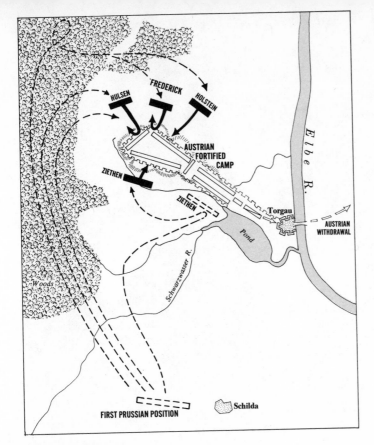

Battle of Torgau

emplaced Austrian cannon before they had time to load. Only about 600 of Frederick's men survived the ordeal of the first attack unwounded.

But at this moment, about 3:00 P.M., Hulsen's column appeared, and Frederick threw them in for a second attack against the same spot in the Austrian defenses. This attack was more successful and captured a number of the Austrian cannon. But Daun, unoccupied elsewhere, was able to bring up reinforce-

Frederick pondering his heavy losses after the Battle of Torgau. (*New York Public Library, Picture Collection*)

ments and again he threw the Prussians back. Frederick was hit by a piece of case shot, and was knocked unconscious. He was not wounded, however, being protected by his fur-lined coat. He recovered consciousness in time to rally the retreating troops.

Then Holstein's column arrived and a third Prussian attack was begun against the center and right flank of the Austrian line. This blow succeeded in breaking through the entrench-

144

ments, and the early darkness of autumn fell on a scene of confused slaughter. Daun was wounded and carried from the field. His replacement, General Von Bucow, was also wounded and General O'Donnell succeeded to command of the Austrians. The outcome was indecisive and Frederick ordered his troops to bivouac through the freezing night, prepared to continue the struggle at dawn.

Suddenly at 6:00 P.M. Ziethen entered the conflict on the other side of the Austrian camp. Finally he had realized his terrible error, and now, in pitch darkness, he and his men advanced toward the sounds and flashes of firing still going on to the north. This attack took the Austrians completely by surprise. Frederick at once ordered his remaining infantry to renew the attack. Panic-stricken by this unexpected double envelopment, the Austrian army fled.

Despite the darkness, Frederick pursued. He wanted to destroy the Austrian army completely, by driving the survivors into the Elbe. But, without any moonlight to help them, the Prussians were unable to find the fleeing foe. Most of the Austrians were able to reach the far bank of the Elbe.

The Prussians lost 13,120 men, almost one-third of Frederick's army. Austrian losses were 16,000 of whom over 7,000 were prisoners.

The loss of the Battle of Torgau was a terrible shock to the allies. But it did not, as Frederick had hoped, end the war. Both sides were so completely weary, however, that for a while they were incapable of further fighting. Nevertheless, during the winter, mostly because of the grim determination of Czarina

Elizabeth, the allies again planned to invade Prussia the following spring.

Desperate Defense

Despite his victory at Torgau, Frederick, in the spring of 1761, was in the most desperate situation he had yet faced in the war. He could only raise 96,000 men; few of these were adequately trained, and at least half were foreign mercenaries. If the armies of Austria and Russia should combine forces, he knew that he and Prussia would be lost.

But the greatest blow was a political upheaval in England. Shortly after the death of George II—in 1760—Pitt's government was overthrown in May, 1761. The new prime minister, Lord Bute, was determined to end the war, and to stop the British subsidy to Prussia without which Frederick could not support his army.

By spring, the allies had 70,000 Austrians and 60,000 Russians in Bohemia and Poland. The main bodies of the allied armies tried to join in Silesia, but Frederick prevented this juncture, threatening first one and then the other. Until midsummer, however, both sides were content with maneuvering; there had been a few skirmishes, but no major battles.

In August, Frederick was still between the two allied armies. He constructed a fortified camp at Bunzelwitz, between the fortresses of Schweidnitz and Striegau and 20 miles north of Glatz. Situated in a mountainous region of central Silesia, the

Bunzelwitz camp was a natural fortress, improved by elaborate field fortifications extemporized in ten days and nights of frantic effort. The 50,000 Prussians worked in two shifts building a palisade, entrenchments, and a ditch 16 feet deep. It was mined, also, with gun-powder charges under all batteries to be blown up in case of capture.

Interestingly, Frederick's *Instructions* had foreseen that this would be the place to defend if disaster ever forced him to go completely on the defensive. Now he was in that situation, which he had said he would avoid if humanly possible.

Laudon urged the Russian commander, General Alexander Buturlin, to join him in an attack on Bunzelwitz. But Buturlin, who was at Hohenfriedberg, 6 miles away, hesitated, and then refused. Finally, on September 9 the Russian withdrew from his camp. Frederick at once sent a detachment after him to destroy the Russian baggage train.

Frederick then moved out of his entrenchments to Neisse, and Laudon seized Schweidnitz. The Austrian commander, instead of using his superior strength to attack Frederick, worked out a complicated plot to capture the Prussian king. But Frederick was warned and the plot failed.

The Brink of Disaster

The year 1761 ended with both Austrians and Prussians in winter camp. Frederick had lost Saxony and much of Silesia. East Prussia and most of Pomerania were also occupied by enemy forces. But, miraculously, the king and the heart of his nation still survived.

It was now clear that the captured *Instructions* were not helping the allies any more than had the consecrated hat and sword. The book had been published in both German and French that year, and had probably been read by every senior officer in the allied armies. Although the allied plan of campaign had tried to prevent Frederick from carrying out his strategy of tactical offensives within interior lines, the plan had failed. The allies had been unprepared for Frederick's move into the fortified camp at Bunzelwitz, despite the information contained in the formerly secret document. Only the brilliant mind that had conceived the *Instructions* was capable of translating its concepts into effective and successful operational plans and actions.

Events beyond Frederick's control, however, now seemed to doom his gallant defense of Prussia. Lord Bute cut off the English subsidy during the winter and Frederick faced the coming 1762 campaign with only 60,000 men. He had not the means even to pay these troops or to feed them properly. In desperation he negotiated with Turkey and with the Tartars of Crimea, to induce them into a war against Russia and Austria. He was convinced that if these new allies did not join him in the spring of 1762, Prussia was lost. The king, in poor health, his spirits dejected, wrote to his ministers to begin negotiations for peace.

Sudden Victory

Then an event occurred that ended Frederick's anxiety. Czarina Elizabeth of Russia died on January 5, 1762. She was succeeded by her nephew, Peter III.

Peter, a simpleminded young man, had always idolized Frederick and had the greatest respect for all things Prussian. He at once made peace. He recalled the Russian armies from Prussia and Poland and began Prussianizing them. Stating that he would rather by a Prussian general than a czar, he sent Frederick 20,000 men to help in his fight against Austria.

Peace between Prussia and Russia was formalized on May 15 by the Treaty of St. Petersburg; East Prussia was returned to Frederick. An allied diplomat complained: "The King of Prussia is now Emperor of Russia."

The course of the war was completely changed. Sweden concluded peace with Frederick on May 22 in the Treaty of Hamburg. Frederick could now concentrate against the Austrians, while Prince Ferdinand still held off the French. On June 24, Ferdinand and his Prusso-British army routed the French in the Battle of Wilhelmstal, in Westphalia. The war seemed all but won.

Then, just as Frederick was advancing into Silesia, in early July, there was another sudden and dramatic change in Russia. Catherine, with the support of Russian nobles, took the throne away from her simpleminded husband. Briefly she considered declaring war on Prussia. Meanwhile she recalled the Russian corps which had been attached to Frederick's army.

Frederick, however, persuaded Czernichev, the Russian commander, to stay for three days, without fighting, after he received the order to return to Russia. With the Russians standing idly by, Frederick attacked and defeated Daun at Burkersdorf on July 21. The next day the Russians left; Czernichev took with him 15,000 ducats and a gold sword studded with diamonds as tokens of Frederick's appreciation.

Outmaneuvering Daun, Frederick next recaptured Schweidnitz, and steadily advanced into Silesia. In Saxony on October 29 Prince Henry, assisted by Seydlitz, defeated a combined Austrian and Reich army at Freiberg, driving them out of the country. Meanwhile Prince Ferdinand had driven the French across the Rhine, and the Turks were invading Hungary.

Maria Theresa had now had enough. Austria offered to make peace. An armistice was declared in November, and on February 16, 1763, Prussia, Austria, and Saxony signed a peace treaty at the castle of Hubertusburg, near Dresden. Frederick, after three wars, was confirmed in possession of Silesia. He asked for no additional territory. England, in her simultaneous peace treaty with France, at Paris, won North America and India, but gained nothing for Prussia.

But Frederick was satisfied. He had won a war that no one else had believed he could win. He had defeated the four great continental land powers of Europe. He had made his own nation, even though it was close to collapse, the fifth great power of Europe. And he, himself, was the most renowned and respected man in the world.

Frederick and Prussia

Reconstruction

At the end of the Seven Years' War, Frederick was fifty-one. He was physically worn out with severe gout, and he suffered from many ailments resulting from the rigors of the long war. He was bent, wrinkled, and gray.

Despite his exhaustion, the king immediately began a tour of the provinces to see what shape his country was in. He found that the population had declined from about 4,500,000 in 1756 to a little more than 4,000,000 in 1763. In addition to 200,000 soldiers who had died in battle or of disease, many civilians had also died of disease and starvation resulting from the war. Towns were deserted, 13,000 houses completely destroyed. The fields were uncultivated, there were no horses for farming and the economy had come to a standstill. Prussia, Brandenburg, and Silesia were in worse physical shape than was Frederick himself.

The king threw himself into the task of rebuilding the devastated country. He pushed his tired body in peacetime pursuits with the same stubbornness with which he had pursued and attacked superior forces in battle. He distributed seed grain to farmers, and then sent army horses to help them get their lands plowed and crops started. He remitted taxes in Prussia and Silesia for 1763. He managed to stabilize the price of grain in Prussia, when it was fluctuating wildly in every other country, by using his hoarded war reserve funds to buy grain when the price fell, and selling from his storage when the price rose. He encouraged immigrants to come to Prussia to replace the population loss of the war. He reclaimed 100,000 acres of marshland, planted 10,000 new acres of woodland, and started 900 new villages.

In three years the ravages of war were repaired. There were 8,000 new houses in Silesia alone. Prussia continued to prosper, and under Frederick's wise rule was able to avoid the economic depressions which periodically affected the rest of Europe. By frugality, by creating a new tax system, as well as developing the country, Frederick soon had his country solvent, when France and Austria remained near bankruptcy as a result of the war.

Frederick did not entrust governmental administration to others any more than was absolutely necessary. He looked after his country and his people as though he were caring for a huge private estate. He held audiences every day with his subjects. He traveled for several months each year and looked into all details of national life. He believed that people only worked at what belonged to them, and Prussia belonged to him, not to the officials he appointed. He kept his court expenses to a minimum, although he built a modest new palace at Sans Souci (1763–69) "to keep the masons busy."

Partition of Poland

At the end of the Seven Years' War, Frederick set his course in foreign affairs by maintaining an alliance with Russia, which he knew was growing to be a mighty force in European politics. In 1772 he and Catherine, and the new Austrian Emperor Joseph—Maria Theresa's son—settled a dispute over control of Poland by agreeing to divide parts of Poland among their three nations.

Prussia gained West Prussia, with 20,000 square miles and 600,000 people. It was less than the gains of Austria and Russia, but it was fertile farmland. Furthermore it united formerly isolated East Prussia with Brandenburg and Pomerania, helping to assure that Prussia would remain a great power. This acquisition was much more important to Prussia than Silesia, and yet Frederick achieved it without a battle.

Frederick went immediately to inspect his new territory, and began reshaping it along Prussian lines. He abolished serfdom, selected able officials, brought in Prussian farmers, established schools, and instituted orderliness.

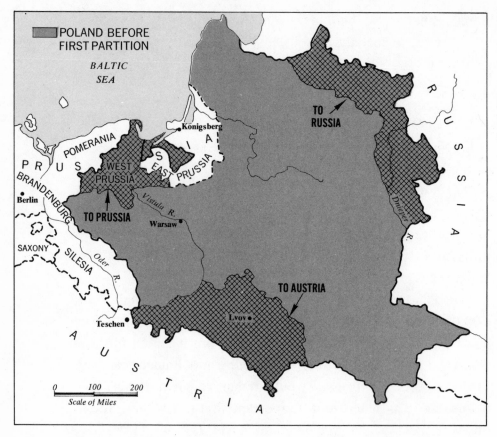

The First Partition of Poland

The Potato War

In 1778 another crisis threatened the peace of Europe. The new Elector of Bavaria surrendered a portion of Lower Bavaria to Austria in return for a cash settlement, and Joseph's Austrian troops occupied this territory.

Frederick was outraged by this Austrian move to increase its power and territory at the expense of a smaller German state. He assembled an army of 100,000 and sent a letter of protest to Joseph. On July 3, 1778, he declared war and marched into Bohemia. An Austrian army soon faced him, but avoided battle. Both forces spent their energies foraging for hay and potatoes and no engagements took place.

In September both Prussians and Austrians withdrew from northern Bohemia because of lack of food in the area. Joseph then withdrew his troops from Bavaria, and in May of 1779 peace was reestablished by the Treaty of Teschen.

One result of the Potato War was to make Frederick the recognized champion of the smaller German princes against the might of Austria. In July of 1785, a League of Princes was formed, representing fourteen German states, with Frederick at its head. The league successfully opposed a new Austrian attempt to take Bavaria. This was the first step toward the unification of Germany under Prussian domination.

Two views of Frederick the Great in old age at Sans Souci. During attacks of gout he was confined to a wheelchair and had to be pushed about the grounds. (Charles Phelps Cushing)

Frederick's Death

Frederick became ever more stubborn in his old age, refusing to give in to his diseases—gout, dropsy, asthma. He also refused to obey his doctors' orders to go on a diet. But his mind was as alert as ever at seventy-three and he continued his administrative duties as well as looking after the army. He was fond of saying that the Prussian people could say what they pleased, and he could do what he pleased.

While reviewing troops in August, 1785, the king sat stubbornly on his horse in a drenching rain for six hours. Next day he had a severe fever and could no longer ride when the fever subsided.

Frederick had himself moved back to Sans Souci and there, for the next year, he continued to work from 4:00 A.M. to 11:00 P.M. daily. He slept sitting up all night to avoid attacks of asthma. He ridiculed his doctors and continued to eat what he wanted, defying their advice and orders.

On August 16, 1786, Frederick did not awaken until afternoon. He could not speak, and could not get up. At 2:20 A.M. the following morning he died in the arms of a devoted orderly, instead of on horseback in battle, as he had always wished.

Chronology

1712,	January 24	Birth of Frederick.
1730,	August 5	Frederick's attempt to escape from Prussia.
	November 6	Execution of Katte.
1733,	June 12	Marriage of Frederick.
1734		Rhine campaign.
1740,	May 31	Death of Frederick William; Frederick II becomes king of Prussia.
	December 16	Frederick invades Silesia; beginning of First Silesian War.
1741,	April 10	Battle of Mollwitz.
	October 9	Agreement of Kleinschnellendorf.
	October 24	France and Bavaria invade Austria; beginning of War of Austrian Succession.
1742,	January 24	Charles Albert of Bavaria is elected emperor.
	February 5	Frederick invades Moravia.

May 17	Battle of Chotusitz.
July 28	Peace of Breslau between Austria and Prussia; end of First Silesian War.
1744, August 15	Frederick invades Bohemia; beginning of Second Silesian War.
September 16	Frederick occupies Prague.
1745, January 8	Union of Warsaw–Anti-Prussian Alliance.
June 4	Battle of Hohenfriedberg.
September 30	Battle of Soor.
December 15	Battle of Kesselsdorf.
December 25	Peace of Dresden; end of Second Silesian War and War of Austrian Succession.
1756, August 29	Frederick invades Saxony; beginning of Seven Years' War.
September 10	Occupation of Dresden.
October 1	Battle of Lobositz.
1757, May 6	Battle of Prague.
June 18	Battle of Kolin.
November 5	Battle of Rossbach.
December 5	Battle of Leuthen.
1758, August 25	Battle of Zorndorf.
October 14	Battle of Hochkirch.
1759, August 1	Battle of Minden.

	August 12	Battle of Kunersdorf.
	November 21	Battle of Maxen.
1760,	August 15	Battle of Liegnitz.
	October 9	Allies capture Berlin.
	November 3	Battle of Torgau.
1761,	August	Encampment at Buntelwitz.
1762,	January 5	Death of Czarina Elizabeth of Russia.
	May 15	Treaty of St. Petersburg—Russia and Prussia.
	July 21	Battle of Burkersdorf.
1763,	February 16	Peace of Hubertusburg; end of Seven Years' War.
1772,	August	First Partition of Poland.
1778–79		The Potato War.
1786,	August 17	Death of Frederick.

Principles of Military Leadership and Military Theory

Since different people have different ideas about leadership and about how it is defined and recognized, a few paragraphs are necessary to explain how the word "leadership" is applied in this book to the military career of one of the outstanding men of history.

Military Leadership

In its simplest terms, *leadership* means the ability of a person to influence and direct other people to work cooperatively together toward a goal or objective, because that individual commands their obedience, confidence, and respect. But these words are really meaningful only if we can relate them to observable standards of performance. One set of standards to show the qualities of a military leader is the following:

Professional military skill or competence. This includes a knowledge and understanding of past military events (or military history), an understanding of theoretical principles of warfare, and a combination of judgment and energy in applying this knowledge and theory to a variety of different situations.

Understanding of the human tools of the leader. This simply means that a leader must know the capabilities and limitations of his men.

Insistence upon high standards of training and discipline. In this way the leader, knowing his men, is able to make the most of their capabilities and to eliminate or reduce their weaknesses and limitations.

Inspirational ability. The leader must be able to project his personality to his men, so that they recognize the quality of his leadership and respond to it with confidence.

Personal courage. The leader must be able to set an example for his men. But in addition to willingness to face the dangers and risks of battle, he must have moral courage off the battle-field to make difficult decisions which lesser men might try to avoid.

Perseverance and determination in adversity. Some men can perform well when everything seems to be going their way. One important measure of human greatness is a person's ability to keep on striving for success, even when his best plans and actions seem to be resulting in failure.

The ability, in peace and war, to understand the relationship between military strategy and national policy. This is as true of a king-general, like Alexander the Great, or a civilian director of war, like Winston Churchill, as it is of the general who is controlled by civilian authority, like George Washington.

These are the seven standards, or yardsticks, of leadership which provide a basis for selecting the great captains. All of these standards are simple, and easy to understand, although their relationship together is so difficult that only a handful of men have been able to measure up close to the maximum of all of these standards.

The reader who is not intimately acquainted with military theory may find some problems with the first of the above standards, in recognizing the ability of a leader to apply military theory and principles to different situations. All that we really need to know, however, to understand the professional military qualities of military leadership which made the great captains great, is the nature of the principles of war and the relationship between strategy and tactics.

Military Theory

Over the past century, military theorists have formulated lists of *Principles of War* which are believed to include all of the fundamental elements of success in waging war. There are some differences among the lists prepared by different theorists, but since they are all based upon review and analysis of historical examples, these various lists are generally consistent with each other. There are differences of opinion as to the applicability of these principles to warfare in the future, but there is no doubt that they provide a useful measurement for past conflicts, since they are derived from, and based upon, the experience of the past.

In this series we use the following list of nine principles of war:

Objective. Every military operation should be directed to accomplish a decisive, realistic objective. The ultimate objective of any conflict is to destroy the enemy's capability and desire to continue the conflict. Intermediate objectives should contribute directly to attaining this ultimate objective. Objectives should be selected after due consideration of the characteristics of the area of conflict, and the resources and military forces which both sides can employ in the conflict.

Offensive. Only offensive action can achieve decisive results, since only by attacking or advancing can a military leader accomplish his objective by forcing his will on the enemy. Sometimes circumstances are such that a commander must take defensive action because the enemy is stronger, or in a more favorable position. But a leader on the defensive should always be seeking to find an opportunity where he can seize the initiative and press toward the achievement of his objective by offensive action. Other principles of war can help him in this search.

Simplicity. A commander must plan his operations and organize his forces so that they are as simple and uncomplicated as possible. When hundreds or thousands of men must work together to accomplish a plan, even the most simple plan may fail. The possibility for confusion and failure is even greater when men and commanders are frightened and excited in the course of a battle.

Control. (This is sometimes called "Unity of Command" or "Cooperation.") There must be one controlling authority to assure the decisive employment of all men and forces toward the achievement of an objective. This controlling authority achieves unity of effort by coordinating the actions of all forces available to him and assures cooperation between all of the individual people or forces engaged in the conflict.

Mass. (This is sometimes called "Concentration.") The maximum available combat power should be applied at the point and at the time which will best assure a decisive success. By seizing the initiative and concentrating forces rapidly and efficiently, a smaller force can often apply greater combat power at the decisive point than a larger enemy force. Mass is not dependent upon numbers alone but results from a combination of manpower, firepower, and fighting capability. Superior weapons, tactics, and morale can contribute to the effectiveness of mass.

Economy of Forces. (This is sometimes called "Economy of Effort.") A commander should employ only the absolute minimum of forces or resources at points which are not decisive. This will permit him to accomplish the principles of the objective and of mass at decisive times and places. Defensive action, or deception, at the less important points will help a commander achieve economy of forces.

Maneuver. Maneuver is the positioning, or the moving, of forces in such a way as to place the enemy at a relative disadvantage. By maneuver a commander can apply the principles of mass and the offensive at a decisive point where the enemy is not adequately prepared or positioned to meet an attack.

Surprise. This is accomplished by striking an enemy at a time, or in a place, or in a manner, that he does not expect. Surprise is particularly important for the commander of a force which does not otherwise have combat superiority to the enemy. Surprise can be achieved by speed, secrecy, deception, variations in fighting methods, and by moving through regions which the enemy does not think are passable for military forces.

Security. This means that a commander must take those measures which will prevent the enemy from surprising him, or from interfering with his operations. With adequate security, a commander can then apply the other principles of war, and employ his own forces in the most effective manner possible.

These principles of war are obviously very general in their nature; they apply to large forces and to small, and to extensive campaigns as well as to brief engagements. Military men usually say that they are applicable to both tactical and strategic operations. This means that the nonmilitary reader should have a clear understanding of the difference between strategy and tactics.

Many, many thousands of words have been written to describe strategy and tactics, and to explain the difference between the two terms. But really the distinction is not difficult.

Military strategy is the art of employing all of the resources available to a military commander for the purpose of achieving a successful outcome in a conflict against hostile armed forces.

Military tactics is the technique of assembling, positioning, and moving some specific portion of the forces available to a commander in order to contribute to the accomplishment of the goals or objectives of strategy.

In other words, strategy concerns the employment and disposition of all means of forces within a commander's power in order to achieve the desired result of a war or campaign. Tactics concerns the specific battlefield methods of employment of these means or forces.

167

Index

171